Selected Poems

By Galway Kinnell

Poetry
What a Kingdom It Was   1960
Flower Herding on Mount Monadnock   1964
Body Rags   1968
First Poems 1946–1954   1971
The Book of Nightmares   1971
The Avenue Bearing the Initial of Christ
   into the New World: Poems 1946–64   1974
Mortal Acts, Mortal Words   1980
Selected Poems   1982

Prose
Black Light   1966
Walking Down the Stairs: Selections from Interviews   1978

Translations
Bitter Victory (Novel by René Hardy)   1956
On the Motion and Immobility of Douve
   (Poems by Yves Bonnefoy)   1968
Lackawanna Elegy (Poems by Yvan Goll)   1970
The Poems of François Villon   1977

GALWAY KINNELL

Selected Poems

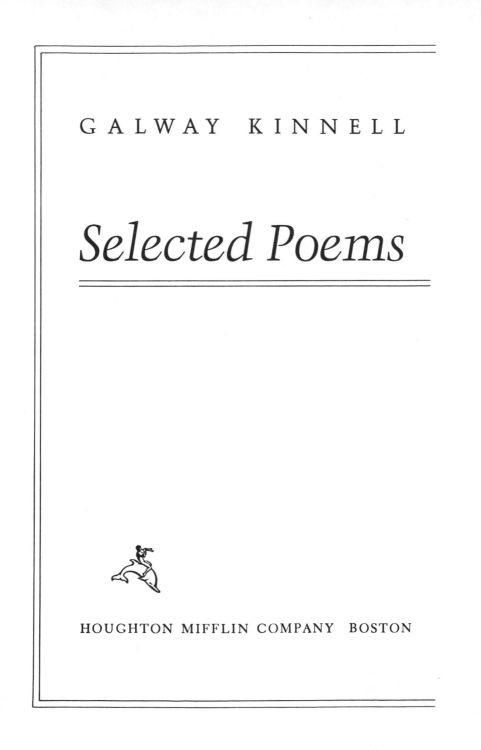

HOUGHTON MIFFLIN COMPANY BOSTON

Library of Congress Cataloging in Publication Data

Kinnell, Galway, (date)
   Selected poems.

   I. Title.
PS3521.I582A6   1982   811'.54   81-20254
ISBN 0-395-32045-3   AACR2
ISBN 0-395-32046-1 pbk.

Printed in the United States of America

V 10 9 8 7

Houghton Mifflin Company paperback 1983

To Roger Nye Lincoln

Contents

FROM

First Poems/1946–1954

Two Seasons

1

The stars were wild that summer evening
As on the low lake shore stood you and I
And every time I caught your flashing eye
Or heard your voice discourse on anything
It seemed a star went burning down the sky.

I looked into your heart that dying summer
And found your silent woman's heart grown wild
Whereupon you turned to me and smiled,
Saying you felt afraid but that you were
Weary of being mute and undefiled.

2

I spoke to you that last winter morning
Watching the wind smoke snow across the ice,
Told how the beauty of your spirit, flesh,
And smile had made day break at night and spring
Burst beauty in the wasting winter's place.

You did not answer when I spoke, but stood
As if that wistful part of you, your sorrow,
Were blown about in fitful winds below:
Your eyes replied your worn heart wished it could
Again be white and silent as the snow.

The Feast

Juniper and cedar in the sand,
The lake beyond, here deer-flesh smoking
On the driftwood fire. And we two
Touching each other by the wash of blue
On the warm sand together lying
As careless as the water on the land.

Now across the water the sunset blooms.
All the pebbles wearing each other
Back into sand speak in the silence;
Or else under the cliff the surf begins,
Telling of another evening, and another,
Beside lapping waters and the small, lapped stones.

The sand turns cold — or the body warms.
If love had not smiled we would never grieve.
But on every earthly place its turning crown
Flashes and fades. We will feast on love again
In the purple light, and rise again and leave
Our two shapes dying in each other's arms.

A Winter Sky

Behind our back the golden woods
Held the gold of a great season
As we lay on the shore of the woods
And watched the long afternoon
Dying in golden light in the woods.

Before us the brown marsh
Brought the dark water, dry grass,
Cattails, waste of the close-cropped marsh,
And the hunters' blinds were watching
For traffic on the blinded marsh.

It had been a long, beautiful fall
And as we sat on the shore remembering
The season behind us, the golden fall,
One of us said to the other
There may never be an end to fall.

Then two ducks flew away from winter
And a gun reached out and caught one
And dropped it like snow in winter,
And without looking back or understanding
The first flew on alone into winter.

We rose as dusky light filled the woods
And looked out over the brown marsh
Where a dog swam and where the fall
Covered the land like a winter
And winter took fall from the marsh and woods.

Meditation Among the Tombs

1

I am kneeling on my grave this lonely
Circle of the day or bottom half
Of night, to witness vainly
Day light candelabra on the dark horizons
Of the world. For this I tell my orisons
And char my tomb with incense for an epitaph.

The present darkness has been long,
And add, the clocks are closing down these days
Lacking a hand to push the hand ahead,
And you will hear the tick and thud
Begin to toil, as the roots of grass
Gnaw decomposition like a cud.

We who have won no issue from our dreams,
Who have never climbed the pale hills of dawn
Nor forged our fullness in the blaze of noon
Nor arched a crimson splendor down the west,
Scowl now at dark — curse God that our best
Is worse than what those grasses chew night-long.

2

Life like a coat of rose-colored paint
Is lifting from his lips. And in those eyes,
Glazed to seal their faint
Flames within, the last red coals
Sputter in his tears. "Try to raise
Your eyelids, gaze upon this cross, for souls
That burn such evil in their fires
Should quench themselves," two preachers hiss in his ears,
"With sorry vows instead of salty tears."

He flutters up those lids, but age
Has so bleared those weary
Eyes and the page

6

On which they register within
That the wrought and polished cross
Those phantoms hold before his chin
Seems but a pole to string its wires high
And shuttle back and forth love's perfidy.

Could such an antique hulk as this
Have ever opened eyes in wonderment of love
Or known the frenzy of a warded kiss?
It is very difficult to think.
And yet it seems he has enough
Old strings and yarns of memory to weave
A gaudy mess of dreams before he leaves.

Look, the glowing caves begin to blink:
What signals do they tell,
What dark suggestion in that skull
That life is twice, compared with death, as terrible?

3

Old Man: When youth was pounding in my veins
 And life was all a sky of light and dreams
 And none had any foresight for the pains
 A girl and I took love in summer's kiss
 Under the oak, half hidden in the grass.
Youth: There must have been much beauty in those flames.

Old Man: Later, when our love burned not so wild
 Or brilliant, but with a steady, subtle fuse
 And she was fevered with a coming child
 They said to me, "Choose you the living wife,
 Or risking her, the babe delivered safe?"
Youth: They might have chosen better word than choose.

Old Man: You who are young have no such memories
 Of trysting by an oak in the thick
 And shining grass, or kissing under skies
 Of singing wind. So which alternative,
 A dead creation or a dying love?
Youth: Creation is a sorry thing to pick.

7

4
Born,
My child, alas, so worn
And old, as though these eyes
Could stuff your sockets with their miseries . . .
I pray
That as your father and his father
Turned the waning cycle of their day,
Bending to the midnight mother
Heaped with age
And bitter with broken rage,
You will wind your days the other
And the better way: and as you near
The end, the furrows of your age will disappear
And everything that prods you to a sudden grave
Will take a counterclockwise turn,
Strange reversal you will learn,
Until your limbs are youthful and your heart is brave.
And having said this prayer,
One word: to life's pretenders say you were
Descended from a line of vanished kings
Who sat in state upon a silver throne —
Then beat from that descent with careless wings
And of their depositions weave your crown.

5

The clock has spun while I have brooded here,
Spading up an earth of long-dead men —
Rain of memory for a rainless year —
Is this a graveyard I am digging in?

But look, the dawn is lighting up the east,
The clouds are breaking, making way — soon!
Now! — through the dusk comes sliding fast,
Alas, that sullen orange eye, the moon.

The clock's two sentinels
Are dying, and midnight has begun again.

Lord, might we witness those castles
Surrender to the fair legions of the sun.

But if the darkness finds the graves where we
Were buried under sillions of our past
Still pointing gloomy crosses at the east,
And thinks that we were niggard with our bravery,
Our ghosts, if such we have, can say at least
We were not misers in our misery.

FROM

What a Kingdom It Was

First Song

Then it was dusk in Illinois, the small boy
After an afternoon of carting dung
Hung on the rail fence, a sapped thing
Weary to crying. Dark was growing tall
And he began to hear the pond frogs all
Calling on his ear with what seemed their joy.

Soon their sound was pleasant for a boy
Listening in the smoky dusk and the nightfall
Of Illinois, and from the fields two small
Boys came bearing cornstalk violins
And they rubbed the cornstalk bows with resins
And the three sat there scraping of their joy.

It was now fine music the frogs and the boys
Did in the towering Illinois twilight make
And into dark in spite of a shoulder's ache
A boy's hunched body loved out of a stalk
The first song of his happiness, and the song woke
His heart to the darkness and into the sadness of joy.

To Christ Our Lord

The legs of the elk punctured the snow's crust
And wolves floated lightfooted on the land
Hunting Christmas elk living and frozen;
Inside snow melted in a basin, and a woman basted
A bird spread over coals by its wings and head.

Snow had sealed the windows; candles lit
The Christmas meal. The Christmas grace chilled
The cooked bird, being long-winded and the room cold.
During the words a boy thought, is it fitting
To eat this creature killed on the wing?

He had killed it himself, climbing out
Alone on snowshoes in the Christmas dawn,
The fallen snow swirling and the snowfall gone,
Heard its throat scream as the gunshot scattered,
Watched it drop, and fished from the snow the dead.

He had not wanted to shoot. The sound
Of wings beating into the hushed air
Had stirred his love, and his fingers
Froze in his gloves, and he wondered,
Famishing, could he fire? Then he fired.

Now the grace praised his wicked act. At its end
The bird on the plate
Stared at his stricken appetite.
There had been nothing to do but surrender,
To kill and to eat; he ate as he had killed, with wonder.

At night on snowshoes on the drifting field
He wondered again, for whom had love stirred?
The stars glittered on the snow and nothing answered.
Then the Swan spread her wings, cross of the cold north,
The pattern and mirror of the acts of earth.

Westport

From the hilltop we could overlook
The changes on the world. Behind us
Spread the forest, that half a continent away
Met our fathers on the Atlantic shore.
Before us lay a narrow belt of brush.
Everywhere beyond, shifting like an ocean,
Swell upon swell of emerald green,
The prairies of the west were blowing.

We mounted and set out, small craft
Into the green. The grasses brushed
The bellies of the horses, and under
The hooves the knotted centuries of sod
Slowed the way. Here and there the gray
Back of a wolf breached and fell, as in the grass
Their awkward voyages appeared and vanished.

Then rain lashed down in a savage squall.
All afternoon it drove us west. "It will be
A hard journey," the boy said, "and look,
We are blown like the weed." And indeed we were . . .
O wild indigo, O love-lies-bleeding,
You, prince's feather, pigweed, and bugseed,
Hold your ground as you can. We toss ahead
Of you in the wild rain, and we barely touch
The sad ambages compassed for yourselves.

When the storm abated, a red streak in the west
Lit up the raindrops on the land before us.
"Yes," I said, "it will be a hard journey . . ."
And the shining grasses were bowed toward the west
As if one craving had killed them. "But at last,"
I added, "the hardness is the thing you thank."
So out of forest we sailed onto plains,
And from the dark afternoon came a bright evening.

Now out of evening we discovered night
And heard the cries of the prairie and the moan
Of wind through the roots of its clinging flowers.

For William Carlos Williams

When you came and you talked and you read with your
Private zest from the varicose marble
Of the podium, the lovers of literature
Paid you the tribute of their almost total
Inattention, although someone when you spoke of a pig
Did squirm, and it is only fair to report another gig-

gled. But you didn't even care. You seemed
Above remarking we were not your friends.
You hung around inside the rimmed
Circles of your heavy glasses and smiled and
So passed a lonely evening. In an hour
Of talking your honesty built you a tower.

When it was over and you sat down and the chair-
man got up and smiled and congratulated
You and shook your hand, I watched a professor
In neat bow tie and enormous tweeds, who patted
A faint praise of the sufficiently damned,
Drained spittle from his pipe, then scrammed.

The Schoolhouse

1

I find it now, the schoolhouse by the tree,
And through the broken door, in brown light,
I see the benches in rows, the floor he
Paced across, the windows where the fruit
Took the shapes of hearts, and the leaves windled
In the fall, and winter snowed on his head.

In this wreck of a house we were taught
Everything we imagined a man could know,
All action, all passion, all ancient thought,
What Socrates had got from Diotima,
How Troilus laughed, in tears, in paradise,
That crowns leapfrog through blood: casts of the dice.

The door hangs from one hinge. Maybe the last
Schoolboy simply forgot to lift the latch
When he rushed out that spring, in his haste —
Or maybe the same one, now fat and rich,
Snow-haired in his turn, and plagued by thought,
Broke his way back in, looking for the dead light.

2

A man of letters once asked the local tramps
To tea. No one came, and he read from Otway
And Chatterton to the walls, and lived for months
On tea. They padlocked the gate when he died.
Snow, sleet, rain, the piss of tramps; and one year
The lock snapped, the gate rasped open like a rooster.

And now when the tramps wake sheeted in frost,
They know it is time, they come here and sprawl
At the foot of the statue of their host
Which they call "His Better Self," which he had called

"Knowledge," sometimes "Death," whose one gesture
Seems to beckon and yet remains obscure,

And boil their tea on the floor and pick fruit
In the garden where that man used to walk
Thinking of Eden and the fallen state,
And dust an apple as he had a book —
"Hey now Porky, gie's the core," one hollers;
"Wise up," says Pork, "they ain't gonna *be* a core."

3
I hear modern schoolchildren shine their pants
In buttock-blessing seats in steamy schools
Soaking up civics and vacant events
From innocents who sponge periodicals
And squeeze that out again in chalky gray
Across the blackboards of the modern day;

Yet they can guess why we fled our benches
Afternoons when we ourselves were just nice
Schoolkids too, who peered out through the branches
For one homely share of the centuries
— Fighting in Latin the wars of the Greeks —
Our green days, the apple we picked and picked

And that was never ours; though they would
Rake their skulls if they found out we returned
By free choice to this house of the dead,
And stand here wondering what he could have learned,
His eyes great pupils and his fishhook teeth
Sunk in the apple of knowledge or death.

4
I recall a recitation in that house:
"*We are the school of Hellas* was the claim.
Maybe it was so. Anyway Hellas
Thought it wasn't, and put the school to flame.
They came back, though, and sifted the ruin."
I think the first inkling of the lesson

Was when we watched him from the apple wrest
Something that put into him the notion
That the earth was coming to its beautifulest
And would be like paradise again
As soon as he died from it. The flames went out
In those blue mantles; he waved us to the night —

And we are here, under the starlight. I
Remember he taught us the stars disperse
In wild flight, though constellated to the eye.
And now I can see the night in its course,
The slow sky uncoiling in exploding forms,
The stars that flee it riding free in its arms.

Freedom, New Hampshire

1

We came to visit the cow
Dying of fever,
Towle said it was already
Shoveled under, in a secret
Burial-place in the woods.
We prowled through the woods
Weeks, we never

Found where. Other
Children other summers
Must have found the place
And asked, Why is it
Green here? The rich
Guess a grave, maybe,
The poor think a pit

For dung, like the one
We shoveled in in the fall
That came up green
The next year, and that,
For all that shows, may as well
Have been the grave
Of a cow or something.

2

We found a cowskull once; we thought it was
From one of the asses in the Bible, for the sun
Shone into the holes through which it had seen
Earth as an endless belt carrying gravel, had heard
Its truculence cursed, had learned how sweat
Stinks, and had brayed — shone into the holes
With solemn and majestic light, as if some
Skull somewhere could be Baalbek or the Parthenon.

That night passing Towle's Barn
We saw lights. Towle had lassoed a calf
By its hind legs, and he tugged against the grip
Of the darkness. The cow stood by chewing millet.
Derry and I took hold, too, and hauled.
It was sopping with darkness when it came free.
It was a bullcalf. The cow mopped it awhile,
And we walked around it with a lantern,

And it was sunburned, somehow, and beautiful.
It took a dug as the first business
And sneezed and drank at the milk of light.
When we got it balanced on its legs, it went wobbling
Toward the night. Walking home in darkness
We saw the July moon looking on Freedom, New Hampshire,
We smelled the fall in the air, it was the summer,
We thought, Oh this is but the summer!

3
Once I saw the moon
Drift into the sky like a bright
Pregnancy pared
From a goddess doomed
To keep slender to be beautiful —
Cut loose, and drifting up there
To happen by itself —
And waning, in lost labor;

As we lost our labor
Too — afternoons
When we sat on the gate
By the pasture, under the Ledge,
Buzzing and skirling on toilet-
papered combs tunes
To the rumble-seated cars
Taking the Ossipee Road

On Sundays; for
Though dusk would come upon us
Where we sat, and though we had
Skirled out our hearts in the music,
Yet the dandruffed
Harps we skirled it on
Had done not much better than
Flies, which buzzed, when quick

We trapped them in our hands,
Which went silent when we
Crushed them, which we bore
Downhill to the meadowlark's
Nest full of throats
Which Derry charmed and combed
With an Arabian air, while I
Chucked crushed flies into

Innards I could not see,
For the night had fallen
And the crickets shrilled on all sides
In waves, as if the grassleaves
Shrieked by hillsides
As they grew, and the stars
Made small flashes in the sky,
Like mica flashing in rocks

On the chokecherried Ledge
Where bees I stepped on once
Hit us from behind like a shotgun,
And where we could see
Windowpanes in Freedom flash
And Loon Lake and Winnipesaukee
Flash in the sun
And the blue world flashing.

4

The fingerprints of our eyeballs would zigzag
On the sky; the clouds that came drifting up
Our fingernails would drift into the thin air;
In bed at night there was music if you listened,
Of an old surf breaking far away in the blood.

Children who come by chance on grass green for a man
Can guess cow, dung, man, anything they want,
To them it is the same. To us who knew him as he was
After the beginning and before the end, it is green
For a name called out of the confusions of the earth —

Winnipesaukee coined like a moon, a bullcalf
Dragged from the darkness where it breaks up again,
Larks which long since have crashed for good in the grass
To which we fed the flies, buzzing ourselves like flies,
While the crickets shrilled beyond us, in July . . .

The mind may sort it out and give it names —
When a man dies he dies trying to say without slurring
The abruptly decaying sounds. It is true
That only flesh dies, and spirit flowers without stop
For men, cows, dung, for all dead things; and it is good, yes —

But an incarnation is in particular flesh
And the dust that is swirled into a shape
And crumbles and is swirled again had but one shape
That was this man. When he is dead the grass
Heals what he suffered, but he remains dead,
And the few who loved him know this until they die.

For my brother, 1925–1957

The Supper After the Last

1

The desert moves out on half the horizon
Rimming the illusory water which, among islands,
Bears up the sky. The sea scumbles in
From its own inviolate border under the sky.
A dragon-fly floating on six legs on the sand
Lifts its green-yellow tail, declines its wings
A little, flutters them a little, and lays
On dazzled sand the shadow of its wings. Near shore
A bather wades through his shadow in the water.
He tramples and kicks it; it recomposes.

2

Outside the open door
Of the whitewashed house,
Framed in its doorway, a chair,
Vacant, waits in the sunshine.

A jug of fresh water stands
Inside the door. In the sunshine
The chair waits, less and less vacant.
The host's plan is to offer water, then stand aside.

3

They eat chicken and *rosé*. The chicken head
Has been tucked under the shelter of the wing.
Under the table a red-backed, passionate dog
Cracks chicken bones on the blood and gravel floor.

No one else but the dog and the blind
Cat watching it knows who is that bearded
Wild man guzzling overhead, the wreck of passion
Emptying his eyes, who has not yet smiled,

Who stares at the company, where he is company,
Turns them to sacks of appalled, grinning skin,
Forks the fowl-eye out from under
The large, makeshift, cooked lid, evaporates the wine,

Jellies the sunlit table and spoons, floats
The deluxe grub down the intestines of the Styx,
Devours all but the cat and the dog, to whom he slips scraps,
The red-backed accomplice busy grinding gristle.

4

When the bones of the host
Crack in the hound's jaw
The wild man rises. Opening
His palms he announces:
I came not to astonish
But to destroy you. Your
Jug of cool water? Your
Hanker after wings? Your
Lech for transcendence?
I came to prove you are
Intricate and simple things
As you are, created
In the image of nothing,
Taught of the creator
By your images in dirt —
As mine, for which you set
A chair in the sunshine,
Mocking me with water!
As pictures of wings,
Not even iridescent,
That clasp the sand
And that cannot perish, you swear,
Having once been evoked!

5

The witnesses back off; the scene begins to float in water;
Far out in that mirage the Saviour sits whispering to the world,

Becoming a mirage. The dog turns into a smear on the sand.
The cat grows taller and taller as it flees into space.

From the hot shine where he sits his whispering drifts:
You struggle from flesh into wings; the change exists.
But the wings that live gripping the contours of the dirt
Are all at once nothing, flesh and light lifted away.

You are the flesh; I am the resurrection, because I am the light.
I cut to your measure the creeping piece of darkness
That haunts you in the dirt. Step into light —
I make you over. I breed the shape of your grave in the dirt.

The Avenue Bearing the Initial of
Christ into the New World

Was diese kleine Gasse doch für ein Reich an sich war . . .

1

pcheek pcheek pcheek pcheek pcheek
They cry. The motherbirds thieve the air
To appease them. A tug on the East River
Blasts the bass-note of its passage, lifted
From the infra-bass of the sea. A broom
Swishes over the sidewalk like feet through leaves.
Valerio's pushcart Ice Coal Kerosene
Moves   clack
                    clack
                              clack
On a broken wheelrim. Ringing in its chains
The New Star Laundry horse comes down the street
Like a roofleak whucking into a pail.
At the redlight, where a horn blares,
The Golden Harvest Bakery brakes on its gears,
Squeaks, and seethes in place. A propane-
gassed bus makes its way with big, airy sighs.

Across the street a woman throws open
Her window,
She sets, terribly softly,
Two potted plants on the windowledge
          tic   tic
And bangs shut her window.

A man leaves a doorway tic toc tic toc tic toc tic hurrah
          toc splat on Avenue C tic etc and turns the corner.
Banking the same corner
A pigeon coasts 5th Street in shadows,
Looks for altitude, surmounts the rims of buildings,
And turns white.

The babybirds pipe down. It is day.

2

In sunlight on the Avenue
The Jew rocks along in a black fur shtraimel,
Black robe, black knickers, black knee-stockings,
Black shoes. His beard like a sod-bottom
Hides the place where he wears no tie.
A dozen children troop after him, barbels flying,
In skullcaps. They are Reuben, Simeon, Levi, Judah, Issachar,
    Zebulun, Benjamin, Dan, Naphtali, Gad, Asher.
With the help of the Lord they will one day become
Courtiers, thugs, rulers, rabbis, asses, adders, wrestlers,
    bakers, poets, cartpushers, infantrymen.

The old man is sad-faced. He is near burial
And one son is missing. The women who bore him sons
And are past bearing, mourn for the son
And for the father, wondering if the man will go down
Into the grave of a son mourning, or if at the last
The son will put his hands on the eyes of his father.

The old man wades toward his last hour.
On 5th Street, between Avenues A and B,
In sunshine, in his private cloud, Bunko Certified Embalmer,
Cigar in his mouth, nose to the wind, leans
At the doorway of Bunko's Funeral Home & Parlour,
Glancing west toward the Ukrainians, eastward idly
Where the Jew rocks toward his last hour.

Sons, grandsons at his heel, the old man
Confronts the sun. He does not feel its rays
Through his beard, he does not understand
Fruits and vegetables live by the sun.
Like his children he is sallow-faced, he sees
A blinding signal in the sky, he smiles.

Bury me not Bunko damned Catholic I pray you in Egypt.

3
From the Station House
Under demolishment on Houston
To the Power Station on 14th,
Jews, Negroes, Puerto Ricans
Walk in the spring sunlight.

The Downtown Talmud Torah
Blosztein's Cutrate Bakery
Areceba Panataria Hispano
Peanuts Dried Fruit Nuts & Canned Goods
Productos Tropicales
Appetizing Herring Candies Nuts
Nathan Kugler Chicken Store Fresh Killed Daily
Little Rose Restaurant
Rubinstein the Hatter Mens Boys Hats Caps Furnishings
J. Herrmann Dealer in All Kinds of Bottles
Natural Bloom Cigars
Blony Bubblegum
Mueren las Cucarachas Super Potente Garantizada de Matar las
    Cucarachas mas Resistentes
Wenig מצבות
G. Schnee Stairbuilder
Everyouth la Original Loción Eterna Juventud Satisfacción Dinero
    Devuelto
Happy Days Bar & Grill

Through dust-stained windows over storefronts
Curtains drawn aside, onto the Avenue
Thronged with Puerto Ricans, Negroes, Jews,
Baby carriages stuffed with groceries and babies,
The old women peer, blessed damozels
Sitting up there young forever in the cockroached rooms,
Eating fresh-killed chicken, productos tropicales,
Appetizing herring, canned goods, nuts;
They puff out smoke from Natural Bloom cigars
And one day they puff like Blony Bubblegum.

From a rooftop a boy fishes at the sky,
Around him a flock of pigeons fountains,
Blown down and swirling up again, seeking the sky.
A red kite wriggles like a tadpole
Into the sky beyond them, crosses
The sun, lays bare its own crossed skeleton.

To fly from this place — to roll
On some bubbly blacktop in the summer,
To run under the rain of pigeon plumes, to be
Tarred, and feathered with birdshit, Icarus,

In Kugler's glass headdown dangling by yellow legs.

4
First Sun Day of the year. Tonight,
When the sun will have turned from the earth,
She will appear outside Hy's Luncheonette,
The crone who sells the *News* and the *Mirror*,
The oldest living thing on Avenue C,
Outdating much of its brick and mortar.
If you ask for the *News* she gives you the *Mirror*
And squints long at the nickel in her hand
Despising it, perhaps, for being a nickel,
And stuffs it in her apron pocket
And sucks her lips. Rain or stars, every night
She is there, squatting on the orange crate,
Issuing out only in darkness, like the cucarachas
And strange nightmares in the chambers overhead.
She can't tell one newspaper from another,
She has forgotten how Nain her dead husband looked,
She has forgotten her children's whereabouts
Or how many there were, or what the *News*
And *Mirror* tell about that we buy them with nickels.
She is sure only of the look of a nickel
And that there is a Lord in the sky overhead.
She dwells in a flesh that is of the Lord
And drifts out, therefore, only in darkness
Like the streetlamp outside the Luncheonette

Or the lights in the secret chamber
In the firmament, where Yahweh himself dwells.
Like Magdalene in the Battistero of Saint John
On the carved-up continent, in the land of sun,
She lives shadowed, under a feeble bulb
That lights her face, her crab's hands, her small bulk on the crate.

She is Pulchería mother of murderers and madmen,
She is also Alyona whose neck was a chicken leg.

Mother was it the insufferable wind?
She sucks her lips a little further into the mousehole.
She stares among the stars, and among the streetlamps.

The mystery is hers.

5

That violent song of the twilight!
Now, in the silence, will the motherbirds
Be dead, and the infantbirds
That were in the dawn merely transparent
Unfinished things, nothing but bellies,
Will they have been shoved out
And in the course of a morning, casually,
On scrawny wings, have taken up the life?

6

In the pushcart market, on Sunday,
A crate of lemons discharges light like a battery.
Icicle-shaped carrots that through black soil
Wove away lie like flames in the sun.
Onions with their shirts ripped seek sunlight
On green skins. The sun beats
On beets dirty as boulders in cowfields,
On turnips pinched and gibbous
From budging rocks, on embery sweets,
On Idahos, Long Islands, and Maines,
On horseradishes still growing weeds on the flat ends,

On cabbages lying about like sea-green brains
The skulls have been shucked from,
On tomatoes, undented plum-tomatoes, alligator-skinned
Cucumbers, that float pickled
In the wooden tubs of green skim milk —

Sky-flowers, dirt-flowers, underdirt-flowers,
Those that climbed for the sun in their lives
And those that wormed away — equally uprooted,
Maimed, lopped, shucked, and misaimed.

In the market in Damascus a goat
Came to a stall where twelve goatheads
Were lined up for sale. It sniffed them
One by one. Finally thirteen goats started
Smiling in their faintly sardonic way.

A crone buys a pickle from a crone,
It is wrapped in the *Mirror*,
At home she will open the wrapping, stained,
And stare and stare and stare at it.

And the cucumbers, and the melons,
And the leeks, and the onions, and the garlic.

7
Already the Avenue troughs the light of day.
Southward, toward Houston and Pitt,
Where Avenue C begins, the eastern ranges
Of the wiped-out lives — punks, lushes,
Panhandlers, pushers, rumsoaks, everyone
Who took it easy when he should have been out failing at some-
    thing —
The pots-and-pans man pushes his cart,
Through the intersection of the light, at 3rd,
Where sunset smashes on the aluminum of it,
On the bottoms, curves, handles, metal panes,
Mirrors: of the bead-curtained cave under the falls
In Freedom, Seekonk Woods leafing the light out,

Halfway to Kingston where a road branched out suddenly,
Between Pamplonne and Les Salins two meeting paths
Over a sea the green of churchsteeple copper.
Of all places on earth inhabited by men
Why is it we find ourselves on this Avenue
Where the dusk gets worse,
And the mirrorman pushing his heaped mirrors
Into the shadows between 3rd and 2nd
Pushes away a mess of old pots and pans?

The ancient Negro sits as usual
Outside the Happy Days Bar & Grill. He wears
Dark glasses. Every once in a while, abruptly,
He starts to sing, chanting in a hoarse, nearly breaking
Voice —

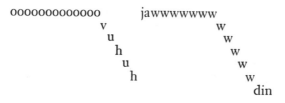

And becomes silent
            Stares into the polaroid Wilderness
Gross-Rosen, Maidanek, Flössenberg, Ravensbruck, Stutthof, Riga,
Bergen-Belsen, Mauthausen, Birkenau, Treblinka, Natzweiler,
Dachau, Buchenwald, Auschwitz —
                                Villages,
Pasture-bordered hamlets on the far side of the river.

8

The promise was broken too freely
To them and to their fathers, for them to care.
They survive like cedars on a cliff, roots
Hooked in any crevice they can find.
They walk Avenue C in shadows
Neither conciliating its Baalim
Nor whoring after landscapes of the senses,

Tarig bab el Amoud being in the blood
Fumigated by Puerto Rican cooking.

Among women girthed like cedar trees
Other, slender ones appear:
One yellow haired, in August,
Under shooting stars on the lake, who
Believed in promises which broke by themselves —
In a German flower garden in the Bronx
The wedding of a child and a child, one flesh
Divided in the Adirondack spring —
One who found in the desert city of the West
The first happiness, and fled therefore —
And by a southern sea, in the pines, one loved
Until the mist rose blue in the trees
Around the spiderwebs that kept on shining,
Each day of the shortening summer.

And as rubbish burns
And the pushcarts are loaded
With fruits and vegetables and empty crates
And clank away on iron wheels over cobblestones,
And merchants infold their stores
And the carp ride motionlessly sleeplessly
In the dark tank in the fishmarket,
The figures withdraw into chambers overhead —
In the city of the mind, chambers built
Of care and necessity, where, hands lifted to the blinds,
They glimpse in mirrors backed with the blackness of the world
Awkward, cherished rooms containing the familiar selves.

9
Children set fires in ashbarrels,
Cats prowl the fires, scraps of fishes burn.

A child lay in the flames.
It was not the plan. Abraham
Stood in terror at the duplicity.
Isaac whom he loved lay in the flames.

The Lord turned away washing
His hands without soap and water
Like a common housefly.

The children laugh.
Isaac means *he laughs*.
Maybe the last instant,
The dying itself, *is* easier,
Easier anyway than the hike
From Pitt the blind gut
To the East River of Fishes,
Maybe it is as the poet said,
And the soul turns to thee
O vast and well-veiled Death
And the body gratefully nestles close to thee —

I think of Isaac reading Whitman in Chicago,
The week before he died, coming across
Such a passage and muttering, Oi!
What shit! And smiling, but not for you — I mean,

For *thee*, Sane and Sacred Death!

10

It was Gold's junkhouse, the one the clacking
Carts that little men pad after in harnesses
Picking up bedbugged mattresses, springs
The stubbornness has been loved out of,
Chairs felled by fat, lampshades lights have burned through,
Linoleum the geometry has been scuffed from,
Carriages a single woman's work has brought to wreck,
Would come to in the dusk and unload before,
That the whole neighborhood came out to see
Burning in the night, flames opening out like
Eyelashes from the windows, men firing the tears in,
Searchlights smashing against the brick,
The water blooming up the walls
Like pale trees, reaching into the darkness beyond.

Nobody mourned, nobody stood around in pajamas
And a borrowed coat steaming his nose in coffee.
It was only Gold's junkhouse.
But this evening
The neighborhood comes out again, everything
That may abide the fire was made to go through the fire
And it was made clean: a few twisted springs,
Charred mattresses (crawling still, naturally),
Perambulator skeletons, bicycles tied in knots —
In a great black pile at the junkhouse door,
Smelling of burnt rubber and hair. Rustwater
Hangs in icicles over the windows and door,
Like frozen piss aimed at trespassers,
Combed by wind, set overnight. Carriages we were babies in,
Springs that used to resist love, that gave in
And were thrown out like whores — the black
Irreducible heap, mausoleum of what we were —
It is cold suddenly, we feel chilled,
Nobody knows for sure what is left of him.

11

The fishmarket closed, the fishes gone into flesh.
The smelts draped on each other, fat with roe,
The marble cod hacked into chunks on the counter,
Butterfishes mouths still open, still trying to eat,
Porgies with receding jaws hinged apart
In a grimace of dejection, as if like cows
They had died under the sledgehammer, perches
In grass-green armor, spotted squeteagues
In the melting ice meek-faced and croaking no more,
Mud-eating mullets buried in crushed ice,
Tilefishes with scales like bits of chickenfat,
Spanish mackerels with buttercups on the flanks,
Pot-bellied pikes, two-tone flounders
After the long contortion of pushing both eyes
To the brown side that they might look up,
Lying brown side down, like a mass laying-on of hands,
Or the oath-taking of an army.

The only things alive are the carp
That drift in the black tank in the rear,
Kept living for the usual reason, that they have not died,
And perhaps because the last meal was garbage and they might
    begin smelling
On dying, before the customer got halfway home.
They nudge each other, to be netted,
The sweet flesh to be lifted thrashing into the air,
To be slugged, and then to keep on living
While they are opened on the counter.

Fishes do not die exactly, it is more
That they go out of themselves, the visible part
Remains the same, there is little pallor,
Only the cataracted eyes that have not shut ever
Must look through the mist which crazed Homer.

These are the vegetables of the deep,
The Sheol-flowers of darkness, swimmers
Of denser darknesses where the sun's rays bend for the last time
And in the sky there burns this shifty jellyfish
That degenerates and flashes and re-forms.

Fishes are nailed to the wood,
The big Jew stands like Christ, nailing them to the wood,
He scrapes the knife up the grain, the scales fly,
He unnails them, reverses them, nails them again,
Scrapes and the scales fly. He lops off the heads,
Shakes out the guts as if they did not belong in the first place,
And they are flesh for the first time in their lives.

Dear Frau ————:

   Your husband, ————, died in the Camp Hospital on ————.
May I express my sincere sympathy on your bereavement. ————
was admitted to the Hospital on ———— with severe symptoms of
exhaustion, complaining of difficulties in breathing and pains in the
chest. Despite competent medication and devoted medical attention,
it proved impossible, unfortunately, to keep the patient alive. The de-
ceased voiced no final requests.

                                        Camp Commandant, ————

38

On 5th Street Bunko Certified Embalmer Catholic
Leans in his doorway drawing on a Natural Bloom Cigar.
He looks up the street. Even the Puerto Ricans are Jews
And the Chinese Laundry closes on Saturday.

12

Next door, outside the pink-fronted Bodega Hispano —

(A crying: you imagine
Some baby in its crib, wailing
As if it could foresee everything.
The crying subsides: you imagine
A mother or father clasping
The damned creature in their arms.
It breaks out again,
This time in a hair-raising shriek — ah,
The alleycat, in a pleasant guise,
In the darkness outside, in the alley,
Wauling slowly in its blood.

Another, loftier shrieking
Drowns it out. It begins always
On the high note, over a clang of bells:
Hook & Ladder 11 with an explosion of mufflers
Crab-walking out of 5th Street,
Accelerating up the Avenue, siren
Sliding on the rounded distances
Returning fainter and fainter,
Like a bee looping away from where you lie in the grass.

The searchlights catch him at the topfloor window,
Trying to move, nailed in place by the shine.

The bells of Saint Brigid's
On Tompkins Square
Toll for someone who has died —
J'oïs la cloche de Serbonne,
Qui tousjours à neuf heures sonne
Le Salut que l'Ange prédit . . .

Expecting the visitation
You lie back on your bed,
The sounds outside
Must be outside. Here
Are only the dead spirituals
Turning back into prayers —
You rise on an elbow
To make sure they come from outside,
You hear nothing, you lay down
Your head on the pillow
Like a pick-up arm —
    swing low
          swing low
               sweet
    lowsweet —)
— Carols of the Caribbean, plinkings of guitars.

13

The garbage-disposal truck
Like a huge hunched animal
That sucks in garbage in the place
Where other animals evacuate it
Whines, as the cylinder in the rear
Threshes up the trash and garbage,
Where two men in rubber suits
(It must be raining outside)
Heap it in. The groaning motor
Rises in a whine as it grinds in
The garbage, and between-times
Groans. It whines and groans again.
All about it as it moves down
5th Street is the clatter of trashcans,
The crashes of them as the sanitary engineers
Bounce them on the sidewalk.

If it is raining outside
You can only tell by looking
In puddles, under the lifted streetlamps.

It would be the spring rain.

40

14

Behind the Power Station on 14th, the held breath
Of light, as God is a held breath, withheld,
Spreads the East River, into which fishes leak:
The brown sink or dissolve,
The white float out in shoals and armadas,
Even the gulls pass them up, pale
Bloated socks of riverwater and rotted seed,
That swirl on the tide, punched back
To the Hell Gate narrows, and on the ebb
Steam seaward, seeding the sea.

On the Avenue, through air tinted crimson
By neon over the bars, the rain is falling.
You stood once on Houston, among panhandlers and winos
Who weave the eastern ranges, learning to be free,
To not care, to be knocked flat and to get up clear-headed
Spitting the curses out. "Now be nice,"
The proprietor threatens; "Be nice," he cajoles.
"Fuck you," the bum shouts as he is hoisted again,
"God fuck your mother." (In the empty doorway,
Hunched on the empty crate, the crone gives no sign.)

That night a wildcat cab whined crosstown on 7th.
You knew even the traffic lights were made by God,
The red splashes growing dimmer the farther away
You looked, and away up at 14th, a few green stars;
And without sequence, and nearly all at once,
The red lights blinked into green,
And just before there was one complete Avenue of green,
The little green stars in the distance blinked.

It is night, and raining. You look down
Toward Houston in the rain, the living streets,
Where instants of transcendence
Drift in oceans of loathing and fear, like lanternfishes,
Or phosphorous flashings in the sea, or the feverish light
Skin is said to give off when the swimmer drowns at night.

From the blind gut Pitt to the East River of Fishes
The Avenue cobbles a swath through the discolored air,
A roadway of refuse from the teeming shores and ghettos
And the Caribbean Paradise, into the new ghetto and new paradise,
This God-forsaken Avenue bearing the initial of Christ
Through the haste and carelessness of the ages,
The sea standing in heaps, which keeps on collapsing,
Where the drowned suffer a C-change,
And remain the common poor.

Since Providence, for the realization of some unknown purpose, has
seen fit to leave this dangerous people on the face of the earth, and
did not destroy it . . .

Listen! the swish of the blood,
The sirens down the bloodpaths of the night,
Bone tapping on the bone, nerve-nets
Singing under the breath of sleep —

We scattered over the lonely seaways,
Over the lonely deserts did we run,
In dark lanes and alleys we did hide ourselves . . .

The heart beats without windows in its night,
The lungs put out the light of the world as they
Heave and collapse, the brain turns and rattles
In its own black axlegrease —

                    In the nighttime
Of the blood they are laughing and saying,
Our little lane, what a kingdom it was!

                    oi weih, oi weih

FROM

Flower Herding
on Mount Monadnock

The River That Is East

1

Buoys begin clanging like churches
And peter out. Sunk to the gunwhales
In their shapes tugs push upstream.
A carfloat booms down, sweeping past
Illusory suns that blaze in puddles
On the shores where it rained, past the Navy Yard,
Under the Williamsburg Bridge
That hangs facedown from its strings
Over which the Jamaica Local crawls,
Through white-winged gulls which shriek
And flap from the water and sideslip in
Over the chaos of illusions, dangling
Limp red hands, and screaming as they touch.

2

A boy swings his legs from the pier,
His days go by, tugs and carfloats go by,
Each prow pushing a whitecap. On his deathbed
Kane remembered the abrupt, missed Grail
Called Rosebud, Gatsby must have flashed back
To his days digging clams in Little Girl Bay
In Minnesota, Nick fished in dreamy Michigan,
Gant had his memories, Griffiths, those
Who went baying after the immaterial
And whiffed its strange dazzle in a blonde
In a canary convertible, who died
Thinking of the Huck Finns of themselves
On the old afternoons, themselves like this boy
Swinging his legs, who sees the *Ile de France*
Come in, and wonders if in some stateroom
There is not a sick-hearted heiress sitting
Drink in hand, saying to herself his name.

3

A man stands on the pier.
He has long since stopped wishing his heart were full
Or his life dear to him.
He watches the snowfall hitting the dirty water.
He thinks: Beautiful. Beautiful.
If I were a gull I would be one with white wings,
I would fly out over the water, explode, and
Be beautiful snow hitting the dirty water.

4

And thou, River of Tomorrow, flowing . . .
We stand on the shore, which is mist beneath us,
And regard the onflowing river. Sometimes
It seems the river stops and the shore
Flows into the past. Nevertheless, its leaked promises
Hopping in the bloodstream, we strain for the future,
Sometimes even glimpse it, a vague, scummed thing
We dare not recognize, and peer again
At the cabled shroud out of which it came,
We who have no roots but the shifts of our pain,
No flowering but our own strange lives.

What is this river but the one
Which drags the things we love,
Processions of debris like floating lamps,
Toward the radiance in which they go out?
No, it is the River that is East, known once
From a high window in Brooklyn, in agony — river
On which a door locked to the water floats,
A window sash paned with brown water, a whiskey crate,
Barrel staves, sun spokes, feathers of the birds,
A breadcrust, a rat, spittle, butts, and peels,
The immaculate stream, heavy, and swinging home again.

To a Child in Calcutta

Dark child in my arms, eyes
The whites of them just like mine
Gazing with black, shined canniness
At mine like large agates in a billboard,

Whom I held as a passerby
A few stricken days down Bandook Gulli,
While they were singing, upstairs,
Everyone in Calcutta is knocking at my door,

You are my conqueror! and you were
Calmly taking in my colored eyes and
Skin burned and thin and
Browned hardly at all by your Bengal sun:

If they show you, when you reach my age,
The blown-up snapshot they took of the stranger
Holding all you once were in his arms,
What will you be able to think, then,

Of the one who came from some elsewhere
And took you in his arms
And let you know the touch of a father
And the old warmth in a paw from nowhere,

But that in his nowhere
He will be dying, letting go his hold
On all for which his heart tore itself
As when they snapped you in his arms like his child,

And going by the photograph
That there was this man, his hair in his eyes,
His hand bigger than your whole head,
Who held you when helplessly

You let him, that between him and you
Were this gesture and this allowance
And he is your stranger father
And he dies in a strange land, which is his own.

In Calcutta, I thought,
Every pimp, taxidriver, whore, and beggar
Dowsed for me through the alleys day and night —
In Bandook Gulli I came upon you,

On a street crossed by fading songs
I held you in my arms
Until you slept, in these arms,
In rags, in the pain of a little flesh.

For Robert Frost

1

Why do you talk so much
Robert Frost? One day
I drove up to Ripton to ask,

I stayed the whole day
And never got the chance
To put the question.

I drove off at dusk
Worn out and aching
In both ears. Robert Frost,

Were you shy as a boy?
Do you go on making up
For some long period of solitude?

Is it simply that talk
Doesn't have to be metered and rhymed?
Or is talk distracting from something worse?

2

I saw you once on the TV,
Unsteady at the lectern,
The flimsy white leaf
Of hair standing straight up
In the wind, among top hats,
Old farmer and son
Of worse winters than this,
Stopped in the first dazzle

Of the District of Columbia,
Suddenly having to pay
For the cheap onionskin,

The worn-out ribbon, the eyes
Wrecked from writing poems
For us — stopped,
Lonely before millions,
The paper jumping in your grip,

And as the Presidents
Also on the platform
Began flashing nervously
Their Presidential smiles
For the harmless old guy,
And poets watching on the TV
Started thinking, Well that's
The end of *that* tradition,

And the managers of the event
Said, Boys this is it,
This sonofabitch poet
Is gonna croak,
Putting the paper aside
You drew forth
From your great faithful heart
The poem.

3

Once, walking in winter in Vermont,
In the snow, I followed a set of footprints
That aimed for the woods. At the verge
I could make out, "far in the pillared dark,"
An old creature in a huge, clumsy overcoat,
Lifting his great boots through the drifts,
Going as if to die among "those dark trees"
Of his own country. I watched him go,

Past a house, quiet, warm and light,
A farm, a countryside, a woodpile in its slow
Smokeless burning, alder swamps ghastly white,
Tumultuous snows, blanker whitenesses,
Into the pathless wood, one eye weeping,

The dark trees, for which no saying is dark enough,
Which mask the gloom and lead on into it,
The bare, the withered, the deserted.

There were no more cottages.
Soft bombs of dust falling from the boughs,
The sun shining no warmer than the moon,
He had outwalked the farthest city light,
And there, clinging to the perfect trees,
A last leaf. What was it?
What was that whiteness? — white, uncertain —
The night too dark to know.

4

He turned. *Love,*
Love of things, duty, he said,
And made his way back to the shelter
No longer sheltering him, the house
Where everything was turning to words,

Where he would think on the white wave,
Folded back, that rides in place on the obscure
Pouring of this life to the sea —
And seal the broken lips
Of darkness with the *mot juste.*

5

Poet of the country of white houses,
Of clearings going out to the dark wall of woods
Frayed along the skyline, you who nearly foreknew
The next lines of poems you suddenly dropped,
Who dwelt in access to that which other men
Have burnt all their lives to get near, who heard
The high wind, in gusts, seething
From far off, headed through the trees exactly
To this place where it must happen, who spent
Your life on the point of giving away your heart
To the dark trees, the dissolving woods,

Into which you go at last, heart in hand, deep in:
When we think of a man who was cursed
Neither with the mystical all-lovingness of Walt Whitman
Nor with Melville's anguish to know and to suffer,
And yet cursed . . . A man, what shall I say,
Vain, not fully convinced he was dying, whose calling
Was to set up in the wilderness of his country,
At whatever cost, a man, who would be his own man,
We think of you. And from the same doorway
At which you lived, between the house and the woods,
We see your old footprints going away across
The great Republic, Frost, up memorized slopes,
Down hills floating by heart on the bulldozed land.

Poem of Night

1

I move my hand over
Slopes, falls, lumps of sight,
Lashes barely able to be touched,
Lips that give way so easily
It's a shock to feel under them
The hard smile of bones.

Muffled a little, barely cloaked,
Zygoma, maxillary, turbinate.

2

I put my hand
On the side of your face,
You lean your head a little
Into my hand — and so,
I know you're a dormouse
Taken up in winter sleep,
A lonely, stunned weight.

3

A cheekbone,
A curved piece of brow,
A pale eyelid
Float in the dark,
And now I make out
An eye, dark,
Wormed with far-off, unaccountable lights.

4

Hardly touching, I hold
What I can only think of
As some deepest of memories in my arms,

Not mine, but as if the life in me
Were slowly remembering what it is.

You lie here now in your physicalness,
This beautiful degree of reality.

5
And now the day, raft that breaks up, comes on.

I think of a few bones
Floating on a river at night,
The starlight blowing in place on the water,
The river leaning like a wave toward the emptiness.

Middle of the Way

1

I wake in the night,
An old ache in the shoulder blades.
I lie amazed under the trees
That creak a little in the dark,
The giant trees of the world.

I lie on earth the way
Flames lie in the woodpile,
Or as an imprint, in sperm, of what is to be.
I love the earth, and always
In its darknesses I am a stranger.

2

6 A.M. Water frozen again. Melted it and made tea. Ate a raw egg and the last orange. Refreshed by a long sleep. The trail practically indistinguishable under 8″ of snow. 9:30 A.M. Snow up to my knees in places. Sweat begins freezing under my shirt when I stop to rest. The woods are filled, anyway, with the windy noise of the first streams. 10:30 A.M. The sun at last. The snow starts to melt off the boughs at once, falling with little ticking sounds. Mist clouds are lying in the valleys. 11:45 A.M. Slow, glittering breakers roll in on the beaches ten miles away, very blue and calm. Odd to see it while sitting in snow. 12 noon. An inexplicable sense of joy, as if some happy news had been transmitted to me directly, by-passing the brain. 2 P.M. From the top of Gauldy I looked back into Hebo valley. Castle Rock sticks into a cloud. A cool breeze comes up from the valley, it is a fresh, earthly wind and tastes of snow and trees. It is not like those transcendental breezes that make the heart ache. It brings happiness. 2:30 P.M. Lost the trail. A woodpecker watches me wade about through the snow trying to locate it. The sun has gone back of the trees. 3:10 P.M. Still hunting for the trail. Getting cold. From an elevation I have an open view to the SE, a world of timberless, white hills, rolling, weirdly wrinkled. Above them a pale half moon. 3:45 P.M. Going on by map and compass. I saw a deer a minute ago, he

55

fled touching down every fifteen feet or so. 7:30 P.M. Made camp near the head of Alder Creek. Trampled a bed into the snow and filled it with boughs. Concocted a little fire in the darkness. Ate pork and beans. A slug or two of whiskey burnt my throat. The night very clear. Very cold. That half moon is up there and a lot of stars have come out among the treetops. The fire has fallen to coals.

3

The coals go out,
The last smoke weaves up
Losing itself in the stars.
This is my first night to lie
In the uncreating dark.

In the heart of a man
There sleeps a green worm
That has spun the heart about itself,
And that shall dream itself black wings
One day to break free into the beautiful black sky.

I leave my eyes open,
I lie here and forget our life,
All I see is we float out
Into the emptiness, among the great stars,
On this little vessel without lights.

I know that I love the day,
The sun on the mountain, the Pacific
Shiny and accomplishing itself in breakers,
But I know I live half alive in the world,
Half my life belongs to the wild darkness.

Ruins Under the Stars

1

All day under acrobat
Swallows I have sat, beside ruins
Of a plank house sunk up to its windows
In burdock and raspberry cane,
The roof dropped, the foundation broken in,
Nothing left perfect but axe-marks on the beams.

A paper in a cupboard talks about "Mugwumps,"
In a V-letter a farmboy in the Marines has "tasted battle . . ."
The apples are pure acid on the tangle of boughs,
The pasture has gone to popple and bush.
Here on this perch of ruins
I listen for the crunch of the porcupines.

2

Overhead the skull-hill rises
Crossed on top by the stunted apple,
Infinitely beyond it, older than love or guilt,
Lie the stars ready to jump and sprinkle out of space.

Every night under those thousand lights
An owl dies, or a snake sloughs its skin,
A man in a dark pasture
Feels a homesickness he does not understand.

3

Sometimes I see them,
The south-going Canada geese,
At evening, coming down
In pink light, over the pond, in great,
Loose, always-dissolving V's —

I go out into the field and listen
To the cold, lonely yelping
Of their tranced bodies in the sky.

4

This morning I watched
Milton Norway's sky-blue Ford
Dragging its ass down the dirt road
On the other side of the valley.

Later, off in the woods
A chainsaw was agonizing across the top of some stump.
A while ago the tracks of a little, snowy,
SAC bomber went crawling across heaven.

What of that little hairstreak
That was flopping and batting about
Deep in the goldenrod —
Did she not know, either, where she was going?

5

Just now I had a funny sensation,
As if some angel, or winged star,
Had been perched nearby.
In the chokecherry bush
There was a twig just ceasing to tremble . . .

The bats come in place of the swallows.
In the smoking heap of old antiques
The porcupine-crackle starts up again,
The bone-saw, the blood music of our sphere,
And up there the stars rustling and whispering.

Spindrift

1

On this tree thrown up
From the sea, its tangle of roots
Letting the wind go through, I sit
Looking down the beach: old
Horseshoe crabs, broken skates,
Sand dollars, sea horses, as though
Only primeval creatures get destroyed,
At chunks of sea-mud still quivering,
At the light as it glints off the water
And the billion facets of the sand,
At the soft, mystical shine the wind
Blows over the dunes as they creep.

2

Sit down
By the clanking shore
Of this bitter, beloved sea,

Pluck sacred
Shells from the icy surf,
Fans of gold light, sunbursts,

Lift one to the sun
As a sign you accept to go
All the way to the shrine of the dead.

3

This little bleached root
Drifted from some other shore,
Cold, practically weightless,
Worn down to the lost grip
It always essentially was,

Keeps at least the shape
Of what it held, and so remains
The hand itself of that gravel,
One of earth's
Wandering icons of "to have."

4

I sit listening
To the surf as it falls,
The power and inexhaustible freshness of the sea,
The suck and inner boom
As a wave tears free and crashes back
In overlapping thunders going away down the beach.

It is the most we know of time,
And it is our undermusic of eternity.

5

I think of how I
Sat by a dying woman
In the glow of her wan, absorbed smile,
Her shell of a hand
Wet and cold in both of mine
Light, nearly out, existing as smoke.

6

Under the high wind
That moans in the grass
And whistles through crabs' claws
I sit holding this little lamp,
This icy fan of the sun.

Across gull tracks
And wind ripples in the sand
The wind seethes. My footprints
Slogging for the absolute
Already begin vanishing.

7
What does he really love,
That old man,
His wrinkled eyes
Tortured by smoke,
Walking in the ungodly
Rasp and cackle of old flesh?

The swan dips her head
And peers at the mystic
In-life of the sea,
The gull drifts up
And eddies toward heaven,
The breeze in his arms . . .

Nobody likes to die
But an old man
Can know
A kind of gratefulness
Toward time that kills him,
Everything he loved was made of it.

Flower Herding on Mount Monadnock

1

I can support it no longer.
Laughing ruefully at myself
For all I claim to have suffered
I get up. Damned nightmarer!

It is New Hampshire out here,
It is nearly the dawn.
The song of the whippoorwill stops
And the dimension of depth seizes everything.

2

The song of a peabody bird goes overhead
Like a needle pushed five times through the air,
It enters the leaves, and comes out little changed.

The air is so still
That as they go off through the trees
The love songs of birds do not get any fainter.

3

The last memory I have
Is of a flower which cannot be touched,

Through the bloom of which, all day,
Fly crazed, missing bees.

4

As I climb sweat gets up my nostrils,
For an instant I think I am at the sea,

One summer off Cap Ferrat we watched a black seagull
Straining for the dawn, we stood in the surf,

Grasshoppers splash up where I step,
The mountain laurel crashes at my thighs.

5

There is something joyous in the elegies
Of birds. They seem
Caught up in a formal delight,
Though the mourning dove whistles of despair.

But at last in the thousand elegies
The dead rise in our hearts,
On the brink of our happiness we stop
Like someone on a drunk starting to weep.

6

I kneel at a pool,
I look through my face
At the bacteria I think
I see crawling through the moss.

My face sees me,
The water stirs, the face,
Looking preoccupied,
Gets knocked from its bones.

7

I weighed eleven pounds
At birth, having stayed on
Two extra weeks in the womb.
Tempted by room and fresh air
I came out big as a policeman
Blue-faced, with narrow red eyes.
It was eight days before the doctor
Would scare my mother with me.

Turning and craning in the vines
I can make out through the leaves
The old, shimmering nothingness, the sky.

8

Green, scaly moosewoods ascend,
Tenants of the shaken paradise,

At every wind last night's rain
Comes splattering from the leaves,

It drops in flurries and lies there,
The footsteps of some running start.

9

From a rock
A waterfall,
A single trickle like a strand of wire,
Breaks into beads halfway down.

I know
The birds fly off
But the hug of the earth wraps
With moss their graves and the giant boulders.

10

In the forest I discover a flower.

The invisible life of the thing
Goes up in flames that are invisible
Like cellophane burning in the sunlight.

It burns up. Its drift is to be nothing.

In its covertness it has a way
Of uttering itself in place of itself,
Its blossoms claim to float in the Empyrean,

A wrathful presence on the blur of the ground.

The appeal to heaven breaks off.
The petals begin to fall, in self-forgiveness.
It is a flower. On this mountainside it is dying.

FROM

Body Rags

Another Night in the Ruins

1

In the evening
haze darkening on the hills,
purple
of the eternal, a last bird
crosses over, *'flop flop,'*
adoring
only the instant.

2

Nine years ago,
in a plane that rumbled all night
above the Atlantic,
I could see, lit up
by lightning bolts jumping out of it,
a thunderhead formed like the face
of my brother, looking nostalgically down
on blue,
lightning-flashed moments of the Atlantic.

3

He used to tell me,
"What good is the day?
On some hill of despair
the bonfire
you kindle can light the great sky —
though it's true, of course, to make it burn
you have to throw yourself in . . ."

4

Wind tears itself hollow
in the eaves of my ruins, ghost-flute
of snowdrifts

that build out there in the dark:
upside-down
ravines into which night sweeps
our torn wings, our ink-spattered feathers.

5
I listen.
I hear nothing. Only
the cow, the cow
of nothingness, mooing
down the bones.

6
Is that a
rooster? He
thrashes in the snow
for a grain. Finds
it. Rips
it into
flames. Flaps. Crows.
Flames
bursting out of his brow.

7
How many nights must it take
one such as me to learn
that we aren't, after all, made
from that bird which flies out of its ashes,
that for a man
as he goes up in flames, his one work
is
to open himself, to *be*
the flames?

Vapor Trail Reflected in the Frog Pond

1

The old watch: their
thick eyes
puff and foreclose by the moon. The young, heads
trailed by the beginnings of necks,
shiver,
in the guarantee they shall be bodies.

In the frog pond
the vapor trail of a SAC bomber creeps,

I hear its drone, drifting, high up
in immaculate ozone.

2

And I hear,
coming over the hills, America singing,
her varied carols I hear:
crack of deputies' rifles practicing their aim on stray dogs
    at night,
sput of cattleprod,
TV groaning at the smells of the human body,
curses of the soldier as he poisons, burns, grinds, and stabs
the rice of the world,
with open mouth, crying strong, hysterical curses.

3

And by rice paddies in Asia
bones
wearing a few shadows
walk down a dirt road, smashed
bloodsuckers on their heels, knowing
the flesh a man throws down in the sunshine
dogs shall eat

and the flesh that is upthrown in the air
shall be seized by birds,
shoulder blades smooth, unmarked by old feather-holes,
hands rivered
by blue, erratic wanderings of the blood,
eyes crinkled up
as they gaze up at the drifting sun that gives us our lives,
seed dazzled over the footbattered blaze of the earth.

The Burn

Twelve years ago I came here
to wander across burnt land,
I had only begun to know
the kind of pain others endure,
I was too full of sorrows.
Now, on the dirt road
that winds beside the Kilchis River
to the sea, saplings
on all the hills, I go deep
into the first forest of Douglas firs
shimmering out of prehistory,
a strange shine up where the tops
shut out the sky, whose roots
feed in the waters of the rainbow trout.
And here, at my feet, in the grain
of a burnt log opened by a riverfall,
the clear
swirls of the creation. At the
San Francisco airport, Charlotte,
where yesterday my arms
died around you like old snakeskins, the puffed
needletracks on your arms
marked how the veins wander.
I see you walking like a somnambulist
through a poppy field, blind
as myself on this dirt road, tiny
flowers brightening about you,
the skills of fire, of fanning
the blossoms until they die,
perfected; only the power to nurture
and make whole, only love,
impossible. The mouth of the river.
On these beaches
the sea throws itself down, in flames.

The Fly

1

The fly
I've just brushed
from my face keeps buzzing
about me, flesh-
eater
starved for the soul.

One day I may learn to suffer
his mizzling, sporadic stroll over eyelid and cheek,
even be glad of his burnt singing.

2

The bee is beautiful.
She is the fleur-de-lis in the flesh.
She has a tuft of the sun on her back.
She brings sexual love to the narcissus flower.
She sings of fulfillment only
and stings and dies.
And everything she ever touches
is opening! opening!

And yet we say our last goodbye
to the fly last,
the flesh-fly last,
the absolute last,
the naked dirty reality of him last.

The Falls

The elemental murmur
as they plunge, *croal, croal,*
and *haish, haish,* over
the ledges,
through stepless wheels
and bare axles, down between
sawmills that have
buckled and slid sideways to their knees . . .

When I fall I would fall to my sounding . . .
the lowly,
unchanged, stillic, rainbowed sounding
of the Barton River Falls.

How Many Nights

How many nights
have I lain in terror,
O Creator Spirit, Maker of night and day,

only to walk out
the next morning over the frozen world
hearing under the creaking of snow
faint, peaceful breaths . . .
snake,
bear, earthworm, ant . . .

and above me
a wild crow crying *'yaw yaw yaw'*
from a branch nothing cried from ever in my life.

Last Songs

1

What do they sing, the last birds
coasting down the twilight,
banking
across woods filled with darkness, their
frayed wings
curved on the world like a lover's arms
which form, night after night, in sleep,
an irremediable absence?

2

Silence. Ashes
in the grate. Whatever it is
that keeps us from heaven,
sloth, wrath, greed, fear, could we only
reinvent it on earth
as song.

The Correspondence School
Instructor Says Goodbye to
His Poetry Students

Goodbye, lady in Bangor, who sent me
snapshots of yourself, after definitely hinting
you were beautiful; goodbye,
Miami Beach urologist, who enclosed plain
brown envelopes for the return of your *very*
"Clinical Sonnets"; goodbye, manufacturer
of brassieres on the Coast, whose eclogues
give the fullest treatment in literature yet
to the sagging-breast motif; goodbye, you in San Quentin,
who wrote, "Being German my hero is Hitler,"
instead of "Sincerely yours," at the end of long,
neat-scripted letters demolishing
the pre-Raphaelites:

I swear to you, it was just my way
of cheering myself up, as I licked
the stamped, self-addressed envelopes,
the game I had
of trying to guess which one of you, this time,
had poisoned his glue. I did care.
I did read each poem entire.
I did say what I thought was the truth
in the mildest words I knew. And now,
in this poem, or chopped prose, not any better,
I realize, than those troubled lines
I kept sending back to you,
I have to say I am relieved it is over:
at the end I could feel only pity
for that urge toward more life
your poems kept smothering in words, the smell
of which, days later, would tingle
in your nostrils as new, God-given impulses
to write.

Goodbye,
you who are, for me, the postmarks again
of shattered towns — Xenia, Burnt Cabins, Hornell —
their loneliness
given away in poems, only their solitude kept.

The Last River

◆

When I cross
on the high, back-reared ferry boat
all burnished brass and laboring pistons
and look at the little tugs and sticklighters
and the great ships from foreign lands
and wave to a deckhand gawking at the new world
of sugar cane and shanties and junked cars
and see a girl by the ferry rail,
the curve the breeze makes down her thigh,
and the green waves lighting up . . .
the cell-block
door crawls open and they fling us a pimp.

◆

The lights dim,
the dirty jokes die out.

Rumble of trailertrucks
on Louisiana 1 . . . I think
of the rides
back from the courthouse in Amite,
down the canyon between
faces smiling from the billboards,
the car filled
with black men who tried to register to vote . . .
Tickfaw . . . Independence . . . Albany . . .

Moan of
a riverboat creeping
upstream . . . yap and screech
of police dogs
attacking the police in their dreams.

Note: "The Last River" is a poem in 27 sections. The selection given here omits
sections 6, 7, 8, 9, 17, 19, 21, 22, 23, and 24.

◆

Under the blue flasher
and the siren's wail, I gazed out,
I remember, at anything,
anything at all of the world . . .
surreal spittoon . . .
glow of EAT . . .
fresh-hit carcass . . . cat . . . coon . . .
polecat . . .

and then lightning flashed,
path strung out a moment across the storm,
bolt of being even made of hellfire
between any strange life and any strange life,
blazed
for those who shudder in their beds
hearing a siren's wail
fading down a dead-ridden highway at night . . .
thump . . . armadillo . . . thump . . . dog . . .

◆

Somebody wakes,
he's got himself a "nightcrawler" — one of those
jokes that come to you in your sleep —
about girls who have "cross-bones"
and can't, consequently,
be entered . . . An argument flares up
as to whether there is, or is not,
a way to circumvent the cross-bone . . .
"Sheee-it! Sheee-it!" the copbeater cries,
and the carthief says, "Jeee-ziz! Jeee-ziz!"
"All right boys," the pimp puts in from time to time,
"What say? Let's get a little fucking sleep."

◆

I turn on the iron bunk . . .
One day in Ponchatoula
when the IC from Chicago crept

into the weeds of the Deep South, and stopped,
I thought I saw three
of my kinsmen from the North
in the drinking car, boozing their way
down to New Orleans,
putting themselves across,
selling themselves,
dishing up soft soap,
plump, manicured, shit-eating, opulent, razor-sharp . . .

Then the train
lurched and pushed on, carrying them off,
Yankee . . . equalitarian . . .
grease in the palm of their golden aspirations.

◆

I remember
the ancient ex-convict
who teaches voter-registration
in his shanty under the levee, standing
in the sun on the dirt road . . .
a crepe myrtle tree,
a passion flower,
a butterfly . . .

In the green, blistered sewer,
beer cans, weeds, plastic flowers,
excrement winged
with green flies.

The dust on the road
swirls up into little wing-shapes, that blow off,
the road made of dust goes down . . .

He smiles,
the air brightens as though ashes
of lightning bolts had been scattered through it.

What is it that makes the human face,
bit of secret,
lighted flesh, open up the earth?

◆

A girl and I are lying
on the grass of the levee. Two
birds whirr overhead. We lie close,
as if having waked
in bodies of glory.

And putting on again
its skin of light, the river
bends into view. We watch it, rising
between the levees, flooding for the sky,
and hear it,
a hundred feet down, pressing its long weight
deeper into the world.

The birds have gone,
we wander slowly homeward, lost
in the history of every step . . .

◆

I am a child
and I am lying face-down
by the Ten Mile River, one-half mud
and one-half piss, that runs
between the Seekonk Woods
and the red mills of Pawtucket
with their thousand windows and one smokestack,
breathing the burnt odor
of old rocks,
watching a bug breaking itself up,
holding
to my eye a bleached catfish
skull I turned up in the grass,
inside it, in the pit of light, a cross,

hearing the hornpout sounding
their horns mournfully deep inside the river.

◆

Across
the dreamlit waters pushes
the flag-topped Plaquemine ferry,
and midway between shore and shore
it sounds its horn, and catfishes
of the Mississippi caterwaul and nose over,
heavy-skulled,
into the flinty, night-smelling depths.

◆

All my life, of rivers
I hear
the longing cries, rut-roar
of shifted wind
on the gongs of beaten water . . .

the Ten Mile of Hornpout,
the Drac hissing in its bed of sand,
the Ruknabad crossed by ghosts of nightingales,
the Passumpsic bursting down its length in spring,
the East River of Fishes, the more haunting for not
    having had a past either,
and this Mississippi coursing down now through the silt of
    all its days,
and the Tangipahoa, snake-cracked, lifting with a little
    rush from the hills and going out in thick, under-
    nourished greenery.

◆

Was there some last
fling at grace in those eddies, some swirl
back toward sweet scraping, out there
where an Illinois cornstalk

drifts, turning the hours,
and the grinned skull of a boy?

The burning fodder dowses down,
seeking the snagged
bodies of the water-buried,
bits
of sainfoin sopped in fire, snuffed from below

down the flesh-dark Tallahatchie,
the bone-colored Pearl.

◆

I wrench
a tassel of moss from a limb
to be my lightning-besom and sweep
the mists from the way.

Ahead of me a boy is singing,

    didn't I ramble
    I rambled
    I rambled all around
    in and out the town
    I rambled
    I rambled till the butcher cut me down . . .

He comes out of the mist,
he tells me his name is Henry David,
he takes my hand and leads me over the plain of crushed
    asphodels.

◆

Down here the air's
so thick with American radio-waves,
with our bare ears we can pick up
the groggy, backcountry announcers
drawling their pitch and hardsell:

to old men forgotten under armies of roaches,
to babies with houseflies for lips and eyelashes,
to young men without future puking up present and past,
to recidivists sentenced deep into the hereafter,
to wineheads only a rusty penknife and self-loathing for
    arms,
to hillbilly boys breaking out in sweat at the anti-sweat
    ads,
to . . .
        "Listen!" says Henry David.
"Sheee-it! Sheee-it!" a cupreous-
throated copbeater's chattering far-off in the trees.

◆

A man comes lurching
toward me with big mirrors for eyes,
"Sammich!" he cries and doubles up in laughter.
I remember him at once, from ten years ago,
in Chicago, on a Sunday
in a park on the death-scented South Side,
in the days before my own life had even begun,
when full of strut and happiness
this person came up and cried, "Sammich!"
and now he says, "A fight,
I was makin' the scene and the fuzz
did blast my fuckin' ass off." He laughs.
He is also crying. He shrinks back. "Hey,"
he calls, "thanks for that sammich that day . . .
fat white bastard . . ."

◆

We come to a river
where many thousands kneel, sucking up
its cloudy water
in a kind of frenzy . . .

"What river is it?" I ask.
"The Mystic River," Henry David says,

"the Healing Stream free to all
that flows from Calvary's Mountain . . . the liquor
that makes you forget . . ."

"And what's over there,
on the far shore?" "That?"
he says, "that's Camp Ground . . ."

I turn to see the police whipping
a child who refuses to be born,
she shrieks
and scrambles for the riverbank
and stands
singing in a floating, gospel wail,
"Oh Death, he is a little man . . ."

"What's it like in Camp Ground?" I ask.

But in the mist I only hear,

   I rambled
   in and out the town
   didn't I ramble
   I rambled . . .

   ◆

My brain rids itself of light,
at last it goes out completely,
slowly
slowly
a tiny cell far within it
lights up:

a man of noble face
sits on the iron bunk, wiping
a pile of knifeblades clean
in the rags of his body.
My old hero. Should I be surprised?

"Hard to wash off . . .
buffalo blood . . . Indian blood . . ." he mutters,
at each swipe singing, *"mein herz! mein herz!"*

"Why you," I ask him,
"You who, in your life, loathed our crimes?"

"Seeking love . . . love
without human blood in it,
that leaps above
men and women, flesh and erections,
which I thought I had found
in a Massachusetts gravel bank one spring . . .
seeking love . . .
failing to know I loved most
my purity . . . *mein herz! mein* fucking *herz!"*

"Hey," somebody
from another cellblock shouts, "What say?
Sleep . . . sleep . . ."

The light goes out. In the darkness
a letter for the blind
arrives in my stunned hands.

Did I come all this way only for this, only
to feel out the world-braille of my complicity,
only to choke down these last poison wafers?

For Galway alone.
I send you my mortality.
Which leans out from itself, to spit on itself.
Which you would not touch.
All you have known.

◆

On one bank
of the last river stands
a black man, on the other

a white man, on the water between
a man of no color,
body of beryl,
face of lightning,
eyes lamps of wildfire,
arms and feet of polished brass.

There will come an agony upon you
beyond any
this nation has known;
and at that time thy people,
given intelligence, given imagination, given love,
    given . . .

Here his voice falters, he drops
to his knees, he is
falling to pieces,
no nose left,
no hair,
no teeth,
limbs dangling from prayer-knots and rags,

waiting by the grief-tree
of the last river.

The Porcupine

1

Fatted
on herbs, swollen on crabapples,
puffed up on bast and phloem, ballooned
on willow flowers, poplar catkins, first
leafs of aspen and larch,
the porcupine
drags and bounces his last meal through ice,
mud, roses and goldenrod, into the stubbly high fields.

2

In character
he resembles us in seven ways:
he puts his mark on outhouses,
he alchemizes by moonlight,
he shits on the run,
he uses his tail for climbing,
he chuckles softly to himself when scared,
he's overcrowded if there's more than one of him per five
    acres,
his eyes have their own inner redness.

3

Digger of
goings across floors, of hesitations
at thresholds, of
handprints of dread
at doorpost or window jamb, he would
gouge the world
empty of us, hack and crater
it
until it is nothing, if that
could rid it of all our sweat and pathos.

Adorer of axe
handles aflow with grain, of arms
of Morris chairs, of hand
crafted objects
steeped in the juice of fingertips,
of surfaces wetted down
with fist grease and elbow oil,
of clothespins that have
grabbed our body-rags by underarm and crotch . . .

Unimpressed — bored —
by the whirl of the stars, by *these*
he's astonished, ultra-
Rilkean angel!

for whom the true
portion of the sweetness of earth
is one of those bottom-heavy, glittering, saccadic
bits
of salt water that splash down
the haunted ravines of a human face.

4
A farmer shot a porcupine three times
as it dozed on a tree limb. On
the way down it tore open its belly
on a broken
branch, hooked its gut,
and went on falling. On the ground
it sprang to its feet, and
paying out gut heaved
and spartled through a hundred feet of goldenrod
before
the abrupt emptiness.

5

The Avesta
puts porcupine killers
into hell for nine generations, sentencing them
to gnaw out
each other's hearts for the
salts of desire.

I roll
this way and that in the great bed, under
the quilt
that mimics this country of broken farms and woods,
the fatty sheath of the man
melting off,
the self-stabbing coil
of bristles reversing, blossoming outward —
a red-eyed, hard-toothed, arrow-stuck urchin
tossing up mattress feathers,
pricking the
woman beside me until she cries.

6

In my time I have
crouched, quills erected,
Saint
Sebastian of the
scared heart, and been
beat dead with a locust club
on the bare snout.
And fallen from high places
I have fled, have
jogged
over fields of goldenrod,
terrified, seeking home,
and among flowers
I have come to myself empty, the rope
strung out behind me
in the fall sun
suddenly glorified with all my blood.

7

And tonight I think I prowl broken
skulled or vacant as a
sucked egg in the wintry meadow, softly chuckling, blank
template of myself, dragging
a starved belly through the lichflowered acres,
where
burdock looses the ark of its seed
and thistle holds up its lost bloom
and rosebushes in the wind scrape their dead limbs
for the forced-fire
of roses.

The Bear

1

In late winter
I sometimes glimpse bits of steam
coming up from
some fault in the old snow
and bend close and see it is lung-colored
and put down my nose
and know
the chilly, enduring odor of bear.

2

I take a wolf's rib and whittle
it sharp at both ends
and coil it up
and freeze it in blubber and place it out
on the fairway of the bears.

And when it has vanished
I move out on the bear tracks,
roaming in circles
until I come to the first, tentative, dark
splash on the earth.

And I set out
running, following the splashes
of blood wandering over the world.
At the cut, gashed resting places
I stop and rest,
at the crawl-marks
where he lay out on his belly
to overpass some stretch of bauchy ice
I lie out
dragging myself forward with bear-knives in my fists.

3

On the third day I begin to starve,
at nightfall I bend down as I knew I would
at a turd sopped in blood,
and hesitate, and pick it up,
and thrust it in my mouth, and gnash it down,
and rise
and go on running.

4

On the seventh day,
living by now on bear blood alone,
I can see his upturned carcass far out ahead, a scraggled,
steamy hulk,
the heavy fur riffling in the wind.

I come up to him
and stare at the narrow-spaced, petty eyes,
the dismayed
face laid back on the shoulder, the nostrils
flared, catching
perhaps the first taint of me as he
died.

I hack
a ravine in his thigh, and eat and drink,
and tear him down his whole length
and open him and climb in
and close him up after me, against the wind,
and sleep.

5

And dream
of lumbering flatfooted
over the tundra,
stabbed twice from within,
splattering a trail behind me,
splattering it out no matter which way I lurch,
no matter which parabola of bear-transcendence,

which dance of solitude I attempt,
which gravity-clutched leap,
which trudge, which groan.

6

Until one day I totter and fall —
fall on this
stomach that has tried so hard to keep up,
to digest the blood as it leaked in,
to break up
and digest the bone itself: and now the breeze
blows over me, blows off
the hideous belches of ill-digested bear blood
and rotted stomach
and the ordinary, wretched odor of bear,

blows across
my sore, lolled tongue a song
or screech, until I think I must rise up
and dance. And I lie still.

7

I awaken I think. Marshlights
reappear, geese
come trailing again up the flyway.
In her ravine under old snow the dam-bear
lies, licking
lumps of smeared fur
and drizzly eyes into shapes
with her tongue. And one
hairy-soled trudge stuck out before me,
the next groaned out,
the next,
the next,
the rest of my days I spend
wandering: wondering
what, anyway,
was that sticky infusion, that rank flavor of blood, that
    poetry, by which I lived?

The Book of Nightmares

Note: "Under the Maud Moon," "The Hen Flower,"
"The Dead Shall Be Raised Incorruptible," "Little
Sleep's-Head Sprouting Hair in the Moonlight," and
"Lastness" are parts I, II, VI, VII, and X, respectively,
of *The Book of Nightmares*, a poem in ten parts.

Under the Maud Moon

1

On the path,
by this wet site
of old fires —
black ashes, black stones, where tramps
must have squatted down,
gnawing on stream water,
unhouseling themselves on cursed bread,
failing to get warm at a twigfire —

I stop,
gather wet wood,
cut dry shavings, and for her,
whose face
I held in my hands
a few hours, whom I gave back
only to keep holding the space where she was,

I light
a small fire in the rain.

The black
wood reddens, the deathwatches inside
begin running out of time, I can see
the dead, crossed limbs
longing again for the universe, I can hear
in the wet wood the snap
and re-snap of the same embrace being torn.

The raindrops trying
to put the fire out
fall into it and are
changed: the oath broken,
the oath sworn between earth and water, flesh and spirit, broken,

to be sworn again,
over and over, in the clouds, and to be broken again,
over and over, on earth.

2

I sit a moment
by the fire, in the rain, speak
a few words into its warmth —
stone saint smooth stone — and sing
one of the songs I used to croak
for my daughter, in her nightmares.

Somewhere out ahead of me
a black bear sits alone
on his hillside, nodding from side
to side. He sniffs
the blossom-smells, the rained earth,
finally he gets up,
eats a few flowers, trudges away,
his fur glistening
in the rain.

The singed grease streams
out of the words, the one
held note
remains — a love-note
twisting under my tongue, like the coyote's bark,
curving off, into a
howl.

3

A round-
cheeked girlchild comes awake
in her crib. The green
swaddlings tear open,
a filament or vestment
tears, the blue
flower opens.

And she who is born,
she who sings and cries,
she who begins the passage, her hair
sprouting out,
her gums budding for her first spring on earth,
the mist still clinging about
her face, puts
her hand
into her father's mouth, to take hold of
his song.

4

It is all over,
little one, the flipping
and overleaping, the watery
somersaulting alone in the oneness
under the hill, under
the old, lonely bellybutton
pushing forth again
in remembrance,
the drifting there furled in the dark,
pressing a knee or elbow
along a slippery wall, sculpting
the world with each thrash — the stream
of omphalos blood humming all about you.

5

Her head
enters the headhold
that starts sucking her forth: being itself
closes down all over her, gives her
into the shuddering
grip of departure, the slow,
agonized clenches making
the last molds of her life in the dark.

6

The black eye
opens, the pupil
droozed with black hairs
stops, the chakra
on top of the brain throbs a long moment in world light,

and she skids out on her face into light,
this peck
of stunned flesh
clotted with celestial cheesiness, glowing
with the astral violet
of the underlife. And as they cut

her tie to the darkness
she dies
a moment, turns blue as a coal,
the limbs shaking
as the memories rush out of them. When

they hang her up
by the feet, she sucks
air, screams
her first song — and turns rose,
the slow,
beating, featherless arms
already clutching at the emptiness.

7

When it was cold
on our hillside, and you cried
in the crib rocking
through the darkness, on wood
knifed down to the curve of the smile, a sadness
stranger than ours, all of it
flowing from the other world,

I used to come to you
and sit by you
and sing to you. You did not know,
and yet you will remember,
in the silent zones
of the brain, a specter, descendant
of the ghostly forefathers, singing
to you in the nighttime —
not the songs
of light said to wave
through the bright hair of angels,
but a blacker
rasping flowering on that tongue.

For when the Maud moon
glimmered in those first nights,
and the Archer lay
sucking the icy biestings of the cosmos,
in his crib of stars,

I had crept down
to riverbanks, their long rustle
of being and perishing, down to marshes
where the earth oozes up
in cold streaks, touching the world
with the underglimmer
of the beginning,
and there learned my only song.

And in the days
when you find yourself orphaned,
emptied
of all wind-singing, of light,
the pieces of cursed bread on your tongue,

may there come back to you
a voice,
spectral, calling you
sister!
from everything that dies.

And then
you shall open
this book, even if it is the book of nightmares.

The Hen Flower

1

Sprawled
on our faces in the spring
nights, teeth
biting down on hen feathers, bits of the hen
still stuck in the crevices — if only
we could let go
like her, throw ourselves
on the mercy of darkness, like the hen,

tuck our head
under a wing, hold ourselves still
a few moments, as she
falls out into her little trance in the witchgrass,
or turn over
and be stroked with a finger
down the throat feathers,
down the throat knuckles,
down over the hum
of the wishbone tuning its high D in thin blood,
down over
the breastbone risen up
out of breast flesh, until the fatted thing
woozes off, head
thrown back
on the chopping block, longing only
to die.

2

When the axe-
scented breeze flourishes
about her, her cheeks crush in,
her comb
grays, the gizzard
that turns the thousand acidic millstones of her fate

convulses: ready or not
the next egg, bobbling
its globe of golden earth,
skids forth, ridding her even
of the life to come.

3

Almost high
on subsided gravity, I remain afoot,
a hen flower
dangling from a hand,
wing
of my wing,
of my bones and veins,
of my flesh
hairs lifting all over me in the first ghostly breeze
after death,

wing
made only to fly — unable
to write out the sorrows of being unable
to hold another in one's arms — and unable
to fly,
and waiting, therefore,
for the sweet, eventual blaze in the genes,
that one day, according to gospel, shall carry it back
into pink skies, where geese
cross at twilight, honking
in tongues.

4

I have glimpsed
by corpse-light, in the opened cadaver
of hen, the mass of tiny,
unborn eggs, each getting
tinier and yellower as it reaches back toward
the icy pulp
of what is, I have felt the zero
freeze itself around the finger dipped slowly in.

5

When the Northern Lights
were opening across the black sky and vanishing,
lighting themselves up
so completely they were vanishing,
I put to my eye the lucent
section of the spealbone of a ram —

I thought suddenly
I could read the cosmos spelling itself,
the huge broken letters
shuddering across the black sky and vanishing,

and in a moment,
in the twinkling of an eye, it came to me
the mockingbird would sing all her nights the cry of the rifle,
the tree would hold the bones of the sniper who chose not to
    climb down,
the rose would bloom no one would see it,
the chameleon longing to be changed would remain the color
    of blood.

And I went up
to the henhouse, and took up
the hen killed by weasels, and lugged
the sucked
carcass into first light. And when I hoisted
her up among the young pines, a last
rubbery egg slipping out as I flung her high, didn't it happen
the dead
wings creaked open as she soared
across the arms of the Bear?

6

Sprawled face down, waiting
for the rooster to groan out
it is the empty morning, as he groaned out thrice
for the disciple
of stone,
he who crushed with his heel the brain out of the snake,

I remember long ago I sowed
my own first milk
tooth under hen feathers, I planted under hen feathers
the hook
of the wishbone,
which had broken itself so lovingly toward me.

For the future.

It has come to this.

7
Listen, Kinnell,
dumped alive
and dying into the old sway bed,
a layer of crushed feathers all that there is
between you
and the long shaft of darkness shaped as you,
let go.

Even this haunted room
all its materials photographed with tragedy,
even the tiny crucifix drifting face down at the center of the earth,
even these feathers freed from their wings forever
are afraid.

The Dead Shall Be Raised Incorruptible

1

A piece of flesh gives off
smoke in the field —

carrion,
caput mortuum,
orts,
pelf,
fenks,
sordes,
gurry dumped from hospital trashcans.

Lieutenant!
This corpse will not stop burning!

2

"That you Captain? Sure,
sure I remember — I still hear you
lecturing at me on the intercom, *Keep your guns up, Burnsie!*
and then screaming, *Stop shooting, for crissake, Burnsie,*
those are friendlies! But crissake, Captain,
I'd already started, burst
after burst, little black pajamas jumping
and falling . . . and remember that pilot
who'd bailed out over the North,
how I shredded him down to catgut on his strings?
one of his slant eyes, a piece
of his smile, sail past me
every night right after the sleeping pill . . .

"It was only
that I loved the *sound*
of them, I guess I just loved
the *feel* of them sparkin' off my hands . . ."

3
On the television screen:

Do you have a body that sweats?
Sweat that has odor?
False teeth clanging into your breakfast?
Case of the dread?
Headache so steady it may outlive you?
Armpits sprouting hair?
Piles so huge you don't need a chair to sit at a table?

We shall not all sleep, but we shall be changed . . .

4
In the Twentieth Century of my trespass on earth,
having exterminated one billion heathens,
heretics, Jews, Moslems, witches, mystical seekers,
black men, Asians, and Christian brothers,
every one of them for his own good,

a whole continent of red men for living in community,
one billion species of animals for being sub-human,
and ready and eager to take on
the bloodthirsty creatures from the other planets,
I, Christian man, groan out this testament of my last will.

I give my blood fifty parts polystyrene,
twenty-five parts benzene, twenty-five parts good old gasoline,
to the last bomber pilot aloft, that there shall be one acre
in the dull world where the kissing flower may bloom,
which kisses you so long your bones explode under its lips.

My tongue
goes to the Secretary of the Dead
to tell the corpses, "I'm sorry, fellows,
the killing was just one of those things
difficult to pre-visualize."

My soul I leave to the bee
that he may sting it and die, my brain
to the fly, his back the hysterical green color of slime,
that he may suck on it and die, my flesh to the advertising man,
the anti-prostitute, who loathes human flesh for money.

I assign my crooked backbone
to the dice maker, to chop up into dice,
for casting lots as to who shall see his own blood
on his shirt front and who his brother's,
for the race isn't to the swift but to the crooked.

To the last man surviving on earth
I give my eyelids worn out by fear, to wear
in the absolute night of radiation and silence,
so that his eyes can't close, for regret
is like tears seeping through closed eyelids.

I give the emptiness my hand: the little finger picks no more noses,
slag clings to the black stick of the ring finger,
a bit of flame jets from the tip of the fuck-you finger,
the first finger accuses the heart, which has vanished,
on the thumb stump wisps of smoke ask a ride into the emptiness.

In the Twentieth Century of my nightmare
on earth, I swear on my chromium testicles
to this testament
and last will
of my iron will, my fear of love, my itch for money, and my
    madness.

5
In the ditch
snakes crawl cool paths
over the rotted thigh, the toe bones
twitch in the smell of burnt rubber,
the belly
opens like a poison nightflower,
the tongue has evaporated,

the nostril
hairs sprinkle themselves with yellowish-white dust,
the five flames at the end
of each hand have gone out, a mosquito
sips a last meal from this plate of serenity.

And the fly,
the last nightmare, hatches himself.

6

I ran
my neck broken I ran
holding my head up with both hands I ran
thinking the flames
the flames may burn the oboe
but listen buddy boy they can't touch the notes!

7

A few bones
lie about in the smoke of bones.

Membranes,
effigies pressed into grass,
mummy windings,
desquamations,
sags incinerated mattresses gave back to the world,
memories shocked into the mirrors on whorehouse ceilings,
angel's wings
flagged down into the snows of yesteryear,

kneel
on the scorched earth
in the shapes of men and animals:

do not let this last hour pass,
do not remove this last, poison cup from our lips.

And a wind holding
the cries of love-making from all our nights and days
moves among the stones, hunting
for two twined skeletons to blow its last cry across.

Lieutenant!
This corpse will not stop burning!

Little Sleep's-Head Sprouting Hair in the Moonlight

1

You cry, waking from a nightmare.

When I sleepwalk
into your room, and pick you up,
and hold you up in the moonlight, you cling to me
hard,
as if clinging could save us. I think
you think
I will never die, I think I exude
to you the permanence of smoke or stars,
even as
my broken arms heal themselves around you.

2

I have heard you tell
the sun, *don't go down*, I have stood by
as you told the flower, *don't grow old*,
don't die. Little Maud,

I would blow the flame out of your silver cup,
I would suck the rot from your fingernail,
I would brush your sprouting hair of the dying light,
I would scrape the rust off your ivory bones,
I would help death escape through the little ribs of your body,
I would alchemize the ashes of your cradle back into wood,
I would let nothing of you go, ever,

until washerwomen
feel the clothes fall asleep in their hands,
and hens scratch their spell across hatchet blades,
and rats walk away from the cultures of the plague,
and iron twists weapons toward the true north,
and grease refuses to slide in the machinery of progress,
and men feel as free on earth as fleas on the bodies of men,

and lovers no longer whisper to the one beside them in the
dark, O *you-who-will-no-longer-be* . . .

And yet perhaps this is the reason you cry,
this the nightmare you wake crying from:
being forever
in the pre-trembling of a house that falls.

3

In a restaurant once, everyone
quietly eating, you clambered up
on my lap: to all
the mouthfuls rising toward
all the mouths, at the top of your voice
you cried
your one word, *caca! caca! caca!*
and each spoonful
stopped, a moment, in midair, in its withering
steam.

Yes,
you cling because
I, like you, only sooner
than you, will go down
the path of vanished alphabets,
the roadlessness
to the other side of the darkness,
your arms
like the shoes left behind,
like the adjectives in the halting speech
of very old men,
which used to be able to call up the forgotten nouns.

4

And you yourself,
some impossible Tuesday
in the year Two Thousand and Nine, will walk out
among the black stones
of the field, in the rain,

and the stones saying
over their one word, *ci-gît, ci-gît, ci-gît,*

and the raindrops
hitting you on the fontanel
over and over, and you standing there
unable to let them in.

5

If one day it happens
you find yourself with someone you love
in a café at one end
of the Pont Mirabeau, at the zinc bar
where white wine stands in upward opening glasses,

and if you commit then, as we did, the error
of thinking,
one day all this will only be memory,

learn to reach deeper
into the sorrows
to come — to touch
the almost imaginary bones
under the face, to hear under the laughter
the wind crying across the stones. Kiss
the mouth
which tells you, *here,*
here is the world. This mouth. This laughter. These temple bones.

The still undanced cadence of vanishing.

6

In the light the moon
sends back, I can see in your eyes

the hand that waved once
in my father's eyes, a tiny kite
wobbling far up in the twilight of his last look,

and the angel
of all mortal things lets go the string.

7
Back you go, into your crib.

The last blackbird lights up his gold wings: *farewell*.
Your eyes close inside your head,
in sleep. Already
in your dreams the hours begin to sing.

Little sleep's-head sprouting hair in the moonlight,
when I come back
we will go out together,
we will walk out together among
the ten thousand things,
each scratched in time with such knowledge, *the wages*
of dying is love.

Lastness

The skinny waterfalls, footpaths
wandering out of heaven, strike
the cliffside, leap, and shudder off.

Somewhere behind me
a small fire goes on flaring in the rain, in the desolate ashes.
No matter, now, whom it was built for,
it keeps its flames,
it warms
everyone who might wander into its radiance,
a tree, a lost animal, the stones,

because in the dying world it was set burning.

2

A black bear sits alone
in the twilight, nodding from side
to side, turning slowly around and around
on himself, scuffing the four-footed
circle into the earth. He sniffs the sweat
in the breeze, he understands
a creature, a death-creature
watches from the fringe of the trees,
finally he understands
I am no longer here, he himself
from the fringe of the trees watches
a black bear
get up, eat a few flowers, trudge away,
all his fur glistening
in the rain.

And what glistening! Sancho Fergus,
my boychild, had such great shoulders,
when he was born his head

came out, the rest of him stuck. And he opened
his eyes: his head out there all alone
in the room, he squinted with pained,
barely unglued eyes at the ninth-month's
blood splashing beneath him
on the floor. And almost
smiled, I thought, almost forgave it all in advance.

When he came wholly forth
I took him up in my hands and bent
over and smelled
the black, glistening fur
of his head, as empty space
must have bent
over the newborn planet
and smelled the grasslands and the ferns.

3
Walking toward the cliff overhanging
the river, I call out to the stone,
and the stone
calls back, its voice hunting among the rubble
for my ears.

Stop.
As you approach an echoing
cliffside, you sense the line
where the voice calling from stone
no longer answers,
turns into stone, and nothing comes back.

Here, between answer
and nothing, I stand, in the old shoes
flowed over by rainbows of hen-oil,
each shoe holding the bones
which ripple together in the communion
of the step,
and which open out
in front into toes, the whole foot trying
to dissolve into the future.

A clatter of elk hooves.
Has the top sphere
emptied itself? Is it true
the earth is all there is, and the earth does not last?

On the river the world floats by holding one corpse.

Stop.
Stop here.
Living brings you to death, there is no other road.

4
This is the tenth poem
and it is the last. It is right
at the last, that one
and zero
walk off together,
walk off the end of these pages together,
one creature
walking away side by side with the emptiness.

Lastness
is brightness. It is the brightness
gathered up of all that went before. It lasts.
And when it does end
there is nothing, nothing
left,

in the rust of old cars,
in the hole torn open in the body of the Archer,
in river-mist smelling of the weariness of stones,
the dead lie,
empty, filled, at the beginning,

and the first
voice comes craving again out of their mouths.

5

That Bach concert I went to so long ago —
the chandeliered room
of ladies and gentlemen who would never die . . .
the voices go out,
the room becomes hushed,
the violinist
puts the irreversible sorrow of his face
into the opened palm
of the wood, the music begins:

a shower of rosin,
the bow-hairs listening down all their length
to the wail,
the sexual wail
of the back-alleys and blood strings we have lived
still crying,
still singing, from the sliced intestine
of cat.

6

This poem
if we shall call it that,
or concert of one
divided among himself,
this earthward gesture
of the sky-diver, the worms
on his back still spinning forth
and already gnawing away
the silks of his loves, who could have saved him,
this free floating of one
opening his arms into the attitude
of flight, as he obeys the necessity and falls . . .

7
Sancho Fergus! Don't cry!

Or else, cry.

On the body, when it is
laid out, see if you can find
the one flea that is laughing.

FROM

Mortal Acts,
Mortal Words

Fergus Falling

He climbed to the top
of one of those million white pines
set out across the emptying pastures
of the fifties — some program to enrich the rich
and rebuke the forefathers
who cleared it all once with ox and axe —
climbed to the top, probably to get out
of the shadow
not of those forefathers but of this father,
and saw for the first time,
down in its valley, Bruce Pond, giving off
its little steam in the afternoon,

pond where Clarence Akley came on Sunday mornings to cut down
the cedars around the shore, I'd sometimes hear the slow spondees
of his work, he's gone,
where Milton Norway came up behind me while I was fishing and
stood awhile before I knew he was there, he's the one who put the
cedar shingles on the house, some have curled or split, a few have
blown off, he's gone,
where Gus Newland logged in the cold snap of '58, the only man will-
ing to go into those woods that never got warmer than ten below,
he's gone,
pond where two wards of the state wandered on Halloween, the Na-
tional Guard searched for them in November, in vain, the next fall
a hunter found their skeletons huddled together, in vain, they're
gone,
pond where an old fisherman in a rowboat sits, drowning hooked
worms, when he goes he's replaced and is never gone,

and when Fergus
saw the pond for the first time
in the clear evening, saw its oldness down there
in its old place in the valley, he became heavier suddenly
in his bones

the way fledglings do just before they fly,
and the soft pine cracked . . .

I would not have heard his cry
if my electric saw had been working,
its carbide teeth speeding through the bland spruce of our time, or
    burning
black arcs into some scavenged hemlock plank,
like dark circles under eyes
when the brain thinks too close to the skin,
but I was sawing by hand and I heard that cry
as though he were attacked; we ran out,
when we bent over him he said, "Galway, Inés, I saw a pond!"
His face went gray, his eyes fluttered closed a frightening
    moment . . .

Yes — a pond
that lets off its mist
on clear afternoons of August, in that valley
to which many have come, for their reasons,
from which many have gone, a few for their reasons, most not,
where even now an old fisherman only the pinetops can see
sits in the dry gray wood of his rowboat, waiting for pickerel.

After Making Love We Hear Footsteps

For I can snore like a bullhorn
or play loud music
or sit up talking with any reasonably sober Irishman
and Fergus will only sink deeper
into his dreamless sleep, which goes by all in one flash,
but let there be that heavy breathing
or a stifled come-cry anywhere in the house
and he will wrench himself awake
and make for it on the run — as now, we lie together,
after making love, quiet, touching along the length of our bodies,
familiar touch of the long-married,
and he appears — in his baseball pajamas, it happens,
the neck opening so small
he has to screw them on, which one day may make him wonder
about the mental capacity of baseball players —
and flops down between us and hugs us and snuggles himself to sleep,
his face gleaming with satisfaction at being this very child.

In the half darkness we look at each other
and smile
and touch arms across his little, startlingly muscled body —
this one whom habit of memory propels to the ground of his making,
sleeper only the mortal sounds can sing awake,
this blessing love gives again into our arms.

Saint Francis and the Sow

The bud
stands for all things,
even for those things that don't flower,
for everything flowers, from within, of self-blessing;
though sometimes it is necessary
to reteach a thing its loveliness,
to put a hand on its brow
of the flower
and retell it in words and in touch
it is lovely
until it flowers again from within, of self-blessing;
as Saint Francis
put his hand on the creased forehead
of the sow, and told her in words and in touch
blessings of earth on the sow, and the sow
began remembering all down her thick length,
from the earthen snout all the way
through the fodder and slops to the spiritual curl of the tail,
from the hard spininess spiked out from the spine
down through the great broken heart
to the sheer blue milken dreaminess spurting and shuddering
from the fourteen teats into the fourteen mouths sucking and
    blowing beneath them:
the long, perfect loveliness of sow.

Wait

Wait, for now.
Distrust everything if you have to.
But trust the hours. Haven't they
carried you everywhere, up to now?
Personal events will become interesting again.
Hair will become interesting.
Pain will become interesting.
Buds that open out of season will become interesting.
Second-hand gloves will become lovely again;
their memories are what give them
the need for other hands. And the desolation
of lovers is the same: that enormous emptiness
carved out of such tiny beings as we are
asks to be filled; the need
for the new love *is* faithfulness to the old.

Wait.
Don't go too early.
You're tired. But everyone's tired.
But no one is tired enough.
Only wait a little and listen:
music of hair,
music of pain,
music of looms weaving all our loves again.
Be there to hear it, it will be the only time,
most of all to hear
the flute of your whole existence,
rehearsed by the sorrows, play itself into total exhaustion.

Daybreak

On the tidal mud, just before sunset,
dozens of starfishes
were creeping. It was
as though the mud were a sky
and enormous, imperfect stars
moved across it as slowly
as the actual stars cross heaven.
All at once they stopped,
and as if they had simply
increased their receptivity
to gravity they sank down
into the mud; they faded down
into it and lay still; and by the time
pink of sunset broke across them
they were as invisible
as the true stars at daybreak.

The Gray Heron

It held its head still
while its body and green
legs wobbled in wide arcs
from side to side. When
it stalked out of sight,
I went after it, but all
I could find where I was
expecting to see the bird
was a three-foot-long lizard
in ill-fitting skin
and with linear mouth
expressive of the even temper
of the mineral kingdom.
It stopped and tilted its head,
which was much like
a fieldstone with an eye
in it, which was watching me
to see if I would go
or change into something else.

Blackberry Eating

I love to go out in late September
among the fat, overripe, icy, black blackberries
to eat blackberries for breakfast,
the stalks very prickly, a penalty
they earn for knowing the black art
of blackberry-making; and as I stand among them
lifting the stalks to my mouth, the ripest berries
fall almost unbidden to my tongue,
as words sometimes do, certain peculiar words
like *strengths* or *squinched*,
many-lettered, one-syllabled lumps,
which I squeeze, squinch open, and splurge well
in the silent, startled, icy, black language
of blackberry-eating in late September.

There Are Things I Tell to No One

1

There are things I tell to no one.
Those close to me might think
I was sad, and try to comfort me, or become sad themselves.
At such times I go off alone, in silence, as if listening for God.

2

I say "God"; I believe,
rather, in a music of grace
that we hear, sometimes, playing to us
from the other side of happiness.
When we hear it, when it flows
through our bodies, it lets us live
these days lighted by their vanity
worshipping — as the other animals do,
who live and die in the spirit
of the end — that backward-spreading
brightness. And it speaks in notes struck
or caressed or blown or plucked
off our own bodies: *remember*
existence already remembers
the flush upon it you will have been,
you who have reached out ahead
and taken up some of the black dust
we become, souvenir
which glitters already in the bones of your hand.

3

Just as the supreme cry
of joy, the cry of orgasm, also has a ghastliness to it,
as though it touched forward
into the chaos where we break apart, so the death-groan
sounding into us from another direction carries us back
to our first world, so that the one
whose mouth acids up with it remembers
how oddly fearless he felt
at first imagining the dead,
at first seeing the grandmother or grandfather sitting only yesterday
on the once cluttered, now sadly tidy porch,
that little boned body drowsing almost unobserved into the
      agreement to die.

4

Brothers and sisters;
lovers and children;
great mothers and grand fathers
whose love-times have been cut
already into stone; great
grand fœtuses spelling
the past again into the flesh's waters:
can you bless — or not curse —
whatever struggles to stay alive
on this planet of struggles?
The nagleria eating the convolutions
from the black pulp of thought,
or the spirochete rotting down
the last temples of Eros, the last god?

Then the last cry in the throat
or only dreamed into it
by its threads too wasted to cry
will be but an ardent note

of gratefulness so intense
it disappears into that music
which carries our time on earth away
on the great catafalque
of spine marrowed with god's-flesh,
thighs bruised by the blue flower,
pelvis that makes angels shiver to know down here we mortals make
     love with our bones.

5

In this spirit
and from this spirit, I have learned to speak
of these things, which once I brooded on in silence,
these wishes to live
and to die
in gratefulness, if in no other virtue.

For when the music sounds,
sometimes, late at night, its faint
clear breath blowing
through the thinning walls of the darkness,
I do not feel sad, I do not miss the future or need to be comforted.

Yes, I want to live forever.
I am like everyone. But when I hear
that breath coming through the walls,
grace-notes blown
out of the wormed-out bones,
music that their memory of blood
plucks from the straitened arteries,
that the hard cock and soaked cunt
caressed from each other
in the holy days of their vanity,
that the two hearts drummed
out of their ribs together,
the hearts that know everything (and even

the little knowledge they can leave
stays, to be the light of this house),

then it is not so difficult
to go out, to turn and face
the spaces which gather into one sound, I know now, the singing
of mortal lives, waves of spent existence
which flow toward, and toward, and on which we flow
and grow drowsy and become fearless again.

Goodbye

1

My mother, poor woman, lies tonight
in her last bed. It's snowing, for her, in her darkness.
I swallow down the goodbyes I won't get to use,
tasteless, with wretched mouth-water;
whatever we are, she and I, we're nearly cured.

The night years ago when I walked away
from that final class of junior high school students
in Pittsburgh, the youngest of them ran
after me down the dark street. "Goodbye!" she called,
snow swirling across her face, tears falling.

2

Tears have kept on falling. History
has taught them its slanted understanding
of the human face. At each last embrace
the snow brings down its disintegrating curtain.
The mind shreds the present, once the past is over.

In the Derry graveyard where only her longings sleep
and armfuls of flowers go out in the drizzle
the bodies not yet risen must lie nearly forever . . .
"Sprouting good Irish grass," the graveskeeper blarneys,
he can't help it, "A sprig of shamrock, if they were young."

3

In Pittsburgh tonight, those who were young
will be less young, those who were old, more old, or more likely
no more; and the street where Syllest,
fleetest of my darlings, caught up with me
and hugged me and said goodbye, will be empty. Well,

one day the streets all over the world will be empty —
already in heaven, listen, the golden cobblestones have fallen still —
everyone's arms will be empty, everyone's mouth, the Derry earth.
It is written in our hearts, the emptiness is all.
That is how we have learned, the embrace is all.

Memory of Wilmington

Thirty-some years ago, hitchhiking
north on Route 1, I stopped for the night
at Wilmington, Delaware, one of those American cities
that start falling apart before they ever get finished.
I met, I remember, an ancient hobo — I almost remember
his name — at the ferry — now dead,
of course, him,
and also the ferry —
in great-brimmed hat, coat to his knees,
pants dragging the ground, semi-zootish rig
plucked off various clotheslines. I remember

he taught me how to grab a hen
so the dogs won't hear: how to come up on it
from behind, swoop down and swing it up
and whirl it, all in one motion,
breaking the neck, of course, also twisting
silent any cry
for help it might want to utter —

"give," I suppose, would be the idiom.

It doesn't matter.
It doesn't matter
that we ill-roasted our hen over brushwood
or that with the squeamishness
of the young I dismouthed the rawest of it
the fire hadn't so much as warmed and tossed it
behind me into the black waters of Delaware Bay.

After he ate, I remember, the old hobo
— Amos! yes, that was his name! — old Amos sang,
or rather laughed forth a song or two, his voice
creaking out slower and slower,
like the music in old music boxes, when time slows itself down
   in them.

I sat in the last light and listened, there among rocks,
tin cans, feathers, ashes, old stars. This. This.

The next morning the sun was out
when I sailed north on the ferry.
From the rotting landing Amos waved.
I was fifteen, I think. Wilmington then
was far along on its way to becoming a city
and already well advanced on its way back to dust.

The Still Time

I know there is still time —
time for the hands
to open, for the bones of them
to be filled
by those failed harvests of want,
the bread imagined of the days of not having.

Now that the fear
has been rummaged down to its husk,
and the wind blowing
the flesh away translates itself
into flesh and the flesh
gives itself in its reveries to the wind.

I remember those summer nights
when I was young and empty,
when I lay through the darkness
wanting, wanting,
knowing
I would have nothing of anything I wanted —
that total craving
that hollows the heart out irreversibly.

So it surprises me now to hear
the steps of my life following me —
so much of it gone
it returns, everything that drove me crazy
comes back, blessing the misery
of each step it took me into the world;
as though a prayer had ended
and the bit of changed air
between the palms goes free
to become the glitter
on some common thing that inexplicably shines.

And the old voice,
which once made its broken-off, choked, parrot-incoherences,
speaks again,
this time on the palatum cordis,
this time saying there is time, still time,
for one who can groan
to sing,
for one who can sing to be healed.

The Apple Tree

I remember this tree,
its white flowers all unfallen.
It's the fall, the unfallen apples
hold their brightness
a little longer into the blue air, hold the dream
they can be brighter.

We create without turning,
without looking back, without ever
really knowing we create.
Having tasted
the first flower of the first spring
we go on,
we don't turn again
until we touch the last flower of the last spring.

And that day, fondling
each grain one more time, like the overturned hourglass,
we die
of the return-streaming of everything we have lived.

When the fallen apple rolls
into the grass, the apple worm
stops, then goes
all the way through and looks out
at the creation unopposed, the world
made entirely of lovers.

Or else there is no such thing as memory,
or else there are only the empty branches,
only the blossoms upon them,
only the apples,
that still grow full,
that still fail into brightness,
that still invent past their own decay the dream
they can be brighter,

that still
that still

The one who holds still and looks out,
alone
of all of us, that one may die mostly of happiness.

The Milk Bottle

A tiny creature moves
through the tide pool, holding up
its little fortress foretelling
our tragedies; another clamps
itself down to the stone. A sea anemone
sucks at my finger, mildly, I can just
feel it, though it may mean to kill — no,
it would probably say, to eat
and flow, for all these creatures
even half made of stone seem to thrill
to altered existences. As do we ourselves,
who advance so far, then stop, then creep
a little, stop again, suddenly gasp — breath
is the bright shell
of our life-wish encasing us — gasp
it all back in, on seeing that any time
would be OK
to go, to vanish back into things — as when
lovers wake up at night and see
they both are crying and think, *Yes,*
but it doesn't matter, already
we will have lived forever. And yes,
if we could do that: separate out
time from happiness, remove
the molecules scattered
throughout our flesh that remember, skim them off,
throw them at non-conscious things,
who may even crave them . . . It's funny,
I imagine I can actually remember one certain
quart of milk which has just finished clinking
against three of its brethren
in the milkman's great hand and stands,
freeing itself from itself, on the rotting
doorstep in Pawtucket circa 1932,
to be picked up and taken inside
by one in whom time hasn't yet completely

woven all its tangles, and not ever set down . . .
So that here, by the tide pool,
where a sea eagle rings its glass voice
above us, I remember myself back there,
and first dreams easily untangling
themselves rise in me, flow from me in waves,
as if they felt ready now to be fulfilled
out there where there is nothing.
The old bottle will shatter
in the decay of its music, the sea eagle
will cry itself back down into the sea
the sea's creatures transfigure over and over.
And now everything changes. Look:
Ahead of us the meantime is overflowing.
Around us its own almost-invisibility
streams and sparkles over everything.

Flying Home

It is good for strangers
of few nights to love each other
(as she and I did, eighteen years ago,
strangers of a single night)
and merge in natural rapture —
though it isn't exactly *each other*
but through each other some
force in existence they don't acknowledge
yet propitiate, no matter where,
in the least faithful of beds,
and by the quick dopplering of horns
of trucks plunging down Delancey,
and next to the iron rumblings
of outlived technology, subways up for air,
which blunder past every ten minutes
and botch the TV screen in the next apartment,
where the man in his beer
has to get up from his chair over and over
to soothe the bewildered jerking
things dance with internally,
and under the dead-light of neon,
and among the mating of cockroaches,
and *like* the mating of cockroaches
who were etched before the daybreak
of the gods with compulsions to repeat
that drive them, too, to union
by starlight, without will or choice.
It is also good — and harder —
for lovers who live many years together
to feel their way toward
the one they know completely
and don't ever quite know,
and to be with each other
and to increase what light may shine

in their ashes and let it go out
toward the other, and to need
the whole presence of the other
so badly that the two together
wrench their souls from the future
in which each mostly wanders alone
and in this familiar-strange room,
for this night which lives
amid daily life past and to come
and lights it, find they hold,
perhaps shimmering a little,
or perhaps almost spectral, only the loved
other in their arms.

2

Flying home, looking about
in this swollen airplane, every seat
of it squashed full with one of us,
it occurs to me I might be the luckiest
in this planeload of the species;

for earlier,
in the airport men's room, seeing
the middleaged men my age
as they washed their hands after touching
their penises — when it might have been more in accord
with the lost order to wash first, then touch —
peer into the mirror
and then stand back, slightly puzzled,

I could only think
that one looks relieved to be getting away,
that one dreads going where he goes;

while as for me, at the very same moment
I feel regret at leaving
and happiness to be flying home.

3

As this plane dragging
its track of used ozone half the world long
thrusts some four hundred of us
toward places where actual known people
live and may wait,
we diminish down into our seats,
disappeared into novels of lives clearer than ours,
and yet we do not forget for a moment
the life down there, the doorway each will soon enter:
where I will meet her again
and know her again,
dark radiance with, and then mostly without, the stars.

Very likely she has always understood
what I have slowly learned
and which only now, after being away, almost as far away
as one can get on this globe, almost
as far as thoughts can carry — yet still in her presence,
still surrounded not so much by reminders of her
as by things she had already reminded me of,
shadows of her
cast forward and waiting — can I try to express:

that love is hard,
that while many good things are easy, true love is not,
because love is first of all a power,
its own power,
which continually must make its way forward, from night
into day, from transcending union always forward into difficult day.

And as the plane descends, it comes to me,
in the space
where tears stream down across the stars,
tears fallen on the actual earth
where their shining is what we call spirit,
that once the lover
recognizes the other, knows for the first time
what is most to be valued in another,

from then on, love is very much like courage,
perhaps it *is* courage, and even
perhaps
only courage. Squashed
out of old selves, smearing the darkness
of expectation across experience, all of us little
thinkers it brings home having similar thoughts
of landing to the imponderable world,
the transoceanic airliner,
resisting its huge weight down, comes in almost lightly,
to where
with sudden, tiny, white puffs and long, black, rubberish smears
all its tires *know* the home ground.

About the Author

Galway Kinnell lives in Vermont and New York. He has taught in France, Australia, and Iran, as well as at many colleges and universities in this country. He is currently director of the Creative Writing Program at New York University.